Wandering Spark

Copyright 2024 © Kyle V. Robinson

All rights reserved.

Published in the United States by Town-B Press

Town-B Press and the Mountain Footprint design are trademarks of Town-B Press, LLC

This book or any portion thereof may not be reproduced or used in any manner whatsoever without the express written permission of the publisher except for the use of brief quotations in a book review

ISBN 978-1-7327703-3-1

Wandering Spark: A Memoir/ by Kyle V. Robinson

PRINTED IN THE UNITED STATES OF AMERICA

Cover and interior design by Nuno Moreira, NM DESIGN

10 9 8 7 6 5 4 3 2

SECOND EDITION

Wandering Spark

a memoir

Kyle V. Robinson

Town-B Press

Author's Note:

Writing this book I relied on journals, photographs, texts, emails, and my own recollection. I have changed locations and the names of individuals, modified identities and details when necessary to preserve anonymity. The dialogue in the book was created from my memory that evokes the feeling and meaning of what was said at the time. Everything written in the book is as accurate as possible and based on the truth as I experienced it. The views expressed are my opinions.

TO KATE AND KIRK

CONTENTS

Prologue	I
Chapter 1: Mother Doesn't Always Know Best	23
Chapter 2: Drugs, Fighting, and Lawyering	45
Chapter 3: New Friends, Same Old Story	71
Chapter 4: Wherever I Go, There I Am	89
Chapter 5: Company Man	107
Chapter 6: Going Ultra	129
Chapter 7: Home Is Where I Park It	145
Chapter 8: The Sheriff	161
Chapter 9: Rescue Mission	175
Epilogue: Here I Am	195
Acknowledgements	203

PROLOGUE

"Are you really going to buy this van?" Brad asked, inquisitively, furrowing his eyebrows.

Brad was one of my oldest friends. We first met when we were both twelve years old, after my family moved two blocks away from his house in Cuyahoga Falls, Ohio, which is about forty miles south of Cleveland. We walked to school together almost every day. We made home movies together, skateboarded together, and played backyard basketball and football together. As we got older, we got into our fair share of trouble together, too—he and I both spent most of our teenage years at the garage behind our buddy's house where everyone gathered to drink, get high, play cards, and listen to the local bands who were always practicing there. Brad was always more reserved while I was the outgoing one; in high school, he stayed on the straight and narrow, more or less, while I wobbled. When we were seventeen, he drove me to drug rehab so I could turn myself in. That was probably the beginning of our paths diverging for the first time.

Since then, I'd spent the last decade-plus wandering—for college, for jobs, for law school, and to figure out what the hell I wanted to do with my life. When I moved to Cleveland from New York City and realized Brad was living there, I was excited to reconnect with him. I figured we'd pick back up again where we left off, just like the old days. But I was beginning to rethink all of that as we stood together in the parking lot of a car dealership staring at a silver 2012

Ford Transit Connect cargo van shimmering in the hot July sun. This tall, handsome, sensible fellow with thick brown hair, now married with a child, was giving me a strange look that told me not only was he questioning my admittedly rather wacky, seemingly impulsive, decision—he was also questioning what kind of person all those years of wandering had turned me into.

I paused. If I was being honest, I would have to say that I was wondering that about myself, too—at least a little bit. After a few minutes, I simply replied, "Yes." I was definitely serious about buying the van.

In less than two weeks, when Brad would be eating dinner with his family or drinking with friends at his local bar, I would be in the Cascade Range in Washington State—almost 2,500 miles from Cleveland. At that time, this van would essentially be my new home.

I had done my research on the van. And by "research," I mean that I had looked at a lot of Ford Transits for sale online and had test-driven two others. Businesses used these vans for everything from electrical work to delivering flowers. The cargo space was six feet long, four feet wide, and a little over four feet high. It was perfect for hauling small loads—or, as I was planning to do, building a bed in the back and living in it.

There's an entire community of people who live in vans, and doing so is especially popular in the western US and Australia. Living in a van allows people to explore the world in a way that doesn't cost an arm and a leg and gives them a sense of freedom. After feeling like I had stalled out in Cleveland, I was craving both. Plus, why camp when I could literally just sleep wherever I parked? If I got tired, I could just crawl in the back and go to sleep. It seemed simple.

I needed to get out of Ohio and get out quickly. Otherwise, I knew I'd be stuck in the ordinary, "successful" life I had created for myself there, working all week and then drinking my weekends away with old high school friends like Brad. And I couldn't live with myself if I did that. I had convinced myself that this trip would offer something different, a fix, maybe, to everything that was wrong with my life. *It's now or never, Kyle*, I told myself. *If you don't get this van, your life will be the same as everyone else's. Who cares if you're going to be thirty-eight years old and living in a van?* Admittedly, I cared. But I also knew it was society's norms telling me it wasn't the right thing to do. I was going to do it anyway. I bought the van.

To be fair, I felt uneasy when I signed the dotted line for the van. My heart was beating rapidly, and I felt a pain twist the pit of my stomach. *Don't sign*, a voice in the back of my head warned. I almost got up and left the dealership at one point. *This isn't a smart decision. You're trading in a fully paid-off car. You don't need this van. Your life is going well, Kyle. This doesn't make any sense.*

But there was also a part of me that was scared of what would happen if I didn't buy the van. *You can't live the life you've been living. This version of success is not fulfilling. It's not you. There is still more out there in the world that you need to explore. You have this opportunity. Take it!*

By all accounts, I had risen up after stumbling through a difficult childhood, traumatic adolescence, and messy young adulthood to build a successful life for myself. Somehow I had managed to become a licensed attorney and run a thriving business. However, despite all I had accomplished, I still wasn't fulfilled. I still thirsted for more. I didn't feel like a success, and I definitely didn't feel like I was being true to myself or doing everything I was capable of. I wanted to be happy, and my career wasn't making me happy, or at least not as happy as I thought it would. I wasn't done wandering, as it turned out. I thought this van adventure might be the solution to my unhappiness.

Plus, I wasn't completely running away from my life. I was able to travel because the company I had created was entirely online, giving me the freedom to still make money without being chained to a desk. Lawyers have to take courses in order to maintain their licenses, and my company provides those courses through a website. The process is almost completely automated. All I needed was an occasional internet connection and access to a phone.

Also, call it lucky or unlucky, but I didn't have a significant other, a child, or even a pet to spend my time with. It was just me. Most of my friends in the area had real jobs or families. Not many had a lot of time to spend with a bachelor, nor did they want to, for that matter. If my friends did want to hang out, the only thing they wanted to do was drink. And by "drink," I meant get really drunk because they had a "pass" from their significant other and wanted to take full advantage.

I spent my Sunday mornings and afternoons, for example, binge drinking at either the Winking Lizard Tavern—a converted Elks lodge—or Merry Arts Pub and Grille, where all the townies could be found eating the free, overly salted, popcorn and washing it down with a beer. The bars would be packed with sports fans getting drunk, screaming at the TV, and watching their favorite team—usually the Cleveland Browns—lose.

It was on one such day that I realized I needed a change. I grabbed a round of tall Budweisers from the sticky bar and brought them back to the table. "Here ya go," I said, setting the bottles down in the center of the table. "I'm leaving after this round. I don't want to sit here all day and get wasted."

"Why? Don't be a loser. You have nothing better to do," Carl said as he gulped his beer and slammed his glass back down on the table. My friends were the kind of people who called each other losers as a term of endearment—sort of. I had long since gotten used to hearing the insult.

My usual Sunday-morning drinking comrades were Carl and Tommy. Carl was short, chubby, bald, and always giving me shit. Tommy was a heavyset fellow who was always in the mood for a joke, though he didn't give me as much shit as Carl. If I ever tried to engage them in a conversation about life or about becoming a better person, I would get shot down for "being weird." They just wanted to talk about getting laid, making money, and making fun of other people. When we went out, the main point wasn't to watch the game; it was to get drunk. I went along because I "didn't have anything better to do," which was just bullshit I told myself. I used it as an excuse to avoid doing the work to become who I was truly meant to be. I was afraid of who that was and what that would look like—what if it wasn't all it was supposed to be?

I didn't want to get into an argument, but at that moment, I felt like anything would be better than sitting in that smelly bar with them all day, getting blackout drunk and munching on popcorn. I couldn't explain to them that I knew this wasn't what I wanted out of life; they wouldn't have understood, nor would they have been willing to understand. I didn't feel like the drinking or the drinking-related camaraderie added any value to my life. Plus, I felt like shit the next morning, and I didn't like who I was when I got really drunk. I'd say or do things that I would regret in the morning—things I definitely wouldn't have said or done sober, like making fun of someone or taking a hit of a cigarette or a joint. I hated it and I hated myself for doing it.

This particular Sunday was different. After I set down the beers,

I looked around at all the people in the bar drinking and staring at the TV. Thinking to myself, *This isn't living*, I stood up and told Carl and Tommy I was going to the restroom. I didn't want to explain to them I was actually leaving. I didn't want to hear it from them and I knew they really didn't care, as long as I bought my round of drinks. I'd left the bar with thoughts of buying the van dancing in my head.

I knew there were people out there doing more with their lives, doing the things I wanted to be doing. I saw these people on social media running trails, climbing mountains, or just constantly traveling. I understood that social media was no basis for evaluating my life and that it was somewhat of an illusion. Still, it made me realize that there was an entire world to explore and that I wasn't taking advantage of it. And what was I doing instead? Drinking at the bar or lying on my couch watching reruns of *Seinfeld* or *Law and Order*, and knowing that there was much more to life than what I was experiencing. I would tell myself, *You're wasting your life. There has to be more to my life than my couch, TV, and boozing with friends.* But was I actually going to do something about it?

Even though I was lucky enough to have the opportunity to just go on an adventure, it still took me some time to actually give myself permission to do so. When a door is open, it can be surprisingly hard to walk through it, especially when what's waiting on the other side is unknown. The doubts crept in: *You're thirty-eight; this isn't what thirty-eight-year-olds do. You should be buying a house and starting a family. You still have to pay rent; you can't just leave and pay rent on a place you're not living in. You won't be able to focus on your job as much. You might not have internet access everywhere you go. You don't even know where you're going. This is not a sound decision. How are you going to meet a girl when you're not settled down? This trip is something you need to plan for a long time. What will people think?*

I grew up hearing these voices, the ones that constantly said, *You're not good enough. You're not one of the lucky ones. You can't do that. That's not possible. Get a good job, get married, buy a house, have kids, and that's life.* I didn't listen—I rarely did. That was how I had usually lived my entire life: I would hear the doubts and either pay no attention to them or let them fuel me to do the impossible, just to prove I could.

Even after I bought the van, I still didn't have a solid plan; going out west was as far as I had gotten. I didn't know how long I would be gone. I knew I would eventually have to come back to Ohio, because I had an apartment there with my belongings in it. Though, to be fair, all I really had of value was my TV, one of the things I was trying to get away from.

When I thought about the trip and what would make me happy, I always came back to my love of trail running and ultra-marathons. An ultra-marathon is any race whose distance is longer than 26.2 miles. Some common ultra-marathon distances are 50 kilometers (31.1 miles), 100 kilometers (62.2 miles), 100 miles, and even 200 miles and beyond. Because these types of races don't bring big crowds or money, it's more of a community of runners helping each other out than a competitive environment. Ultra-marathons can take place on any surface—road, trail, or track—though trail running was my preference.

What could be a better way to explore nature and find my tribe than spending some time around ultra-marathon races? Being out on the trails filled my heart with peace and excitement. Plus, all the best trail races are out west, and they're always looking for volunteers to work aid stations, hand out food and water; organize parking; check runners in; mark the course; and so on. Volunteering at races would give me a destination, something to do, and a way to meet people who were in the same community. My decision was made: I would volunteer at an ultra-marathon race out west and meet my peeps.

As I searched for volunteer opportunities with ultras, I came across a race in the Cascade Range in Washington State, specifically in the Gifford Pinchot National Forest. This wasn't a typical ultra-marathon; this race took place near the iconic Mount Saint Helens. The race started at Mount Saint Helens in the Cascades and finished in Randle, Washington, traversing the mountains. The course had more than 42,000 feet of ascent and more than 96,000 feet of elevation change.

It wasn't a stage race, either. Stage races are divided into several parts, or legs, and may have more than one participant on a team doing a leg. They often take place over the course of several days or even weeks, with rest days built in for the participants. This race, on the other hand, was a solitary nonstop run. All runners received when they finished was a belt buckle and the satisfaction of completion. There was no prize money or fanfare. That was part of the appeal.

The race in the Cascades was looking for volunteers to help mark the course and help out with the race. Races that take place over long distances, especially on trails, need to be well marked beforehand so runners don't get lost. The marking is done by "fast packing"—circumnavigating the entire route with a backpack as fast as possible to place flags, markers, dragons, stakes, and signs to direct the runners along the course. Course marking was an ideal option for me because I would get to see the entire course and the surrounding landscape and also get some exercise. It seemed like exactly the kind of adventure I was looking for.

I emailed the volunteer organizers, Paul and Robin. I offered to help out at the race and told them I'd meet them in Washington in late July or early August. They quickly emailed me back and accepted my offer to come mark the course. They informed me they would already be course-marking by the time I arrived in Washington and I should plan to meet them on the mountain. We would rendezvous at Elk Pass, a trailhead near Mount Saint Helens, about forty-five minutes outside of Randle.

I bought the van shortly after I emailed Paul and Robin and two weeks before I left to meet up with them. Before I left, though, I needed to convert the van so that I would be able to sleep in it whenever I wanted. This process proved to be both crazy and expensive. People often turn these vans into literal homes, with running water, ovens, microwaves, and toilets, and they spend tens of thousands of dollars doing this conversion. I would have loved to do that—though without spending the money—but I had less than two weeks. Also, I wasn't exactly sure what I wanted, other than a place to sleep. I told myself that once I got out west, I would figure out what I really wanted in the van and build accordingly later. I knew I wouldn't need a sink with running water, as I had a few gallon jugs. I didn't need a toilet, as I had a pee cup, and to take care of other business, I'd just stop somewhere or hold it. I had no need for an oven or microwave—I had food that didn't need to be cooked, and I could always stop somewhere along the way. All I really needed was a sleeping bag, a book, my journal, my phone, and my computer.

I found plans for an easy bed conversion online and decided to just go with that. I went to my local Home Depot and bought a bunch of wood and supplies. I feel it is important to note that I do not have one handy bone in my entire body. The good thing is that I can follow directions well, so I hoped these two facets of my personality would balance out.

In the end, the bed I built was nothing spectacular, but it worked. It was basically a wooden box frame that was a little over six feet long and two feet wide. It was about a foot and a half off the floor so I could store supplies underneath it. That wooden bed was where I would be sleeping for the next five months.

The final step in the van-conversion process was to shade or black out the windows. Although the windows were already factory tinted, prying eyes could still see into the van if they really wanted, and I needed more privacy if I was going to make this my home. I bought a roll of reflective insulation and cut it up to fit the shape of each of my windows. Then I spray-painted the reflective pieces black, so when they were against the window, it would look like a very dark tint job and no one could see inside. I also purchased a retractable curtain rod, placed it on the ceiling right behind the front seats, and hung an old set of blue curtains to block the view from the front of the van. With that, my van conversion was complete.

I did, however, still lack in one area: supplies, mainly camping gear. After a few weeks out west, I did finally figure out what was necessary and eventually made a trip to REI, but before that, my initial stock included a leaky Walmart tent borrowed from my brother, a goose-patterned 1960s sleeping bag, a two-gallon cooler, a Walmart butane camping stove, an assortment of camping dishes, a battery-powered fan, two duffel bags of clothes, and my running gear. I also had five pairs of shoes—two pairs of road shoes, trail shoes, casual shoes, and walking shoes—and a Styrofoam cooler. I would quickly regret not bringing my thermal jacket. Because it was summer when I left Cleveland, I didn't realize how cold it could get in the mountains in the Pacific Northwest.

On July 30, 2016, I packed up, fueled up, and took off, heading west in my van. According to Google Maps, my trip from Ohio to Washington would be 2,425 miles long, taking thirty-five hours. With sleep, it would take me almost two full days. The directions took me through the northern parts of the United States via Interstate 90. I was alone, and I wished I had someone to talk to during those hours and hours of driving along the not-so-scenic highway.

Early in my journey, I drove past Chicago and saw the city's skyline with the Willis Tower in the distance. I thought of all the "suits" going to their nine-to-five jobs and smirked. It wasn't until I hit Wisconsin that I began thinking, *What the hell are you doing, Kyle?* I tried not to dwell on that thought and just kept pushing forward. It felt good to have what felt like a healthy destination, to not be scrambling or searching wildly for an escape with only a few dollars in my pocket, as I'd done too many times before. This time, I was confident. I had a goal: to make it out west.

And then? Well, I was about to find out.

CHAPTER 1

Mother Doesn't Always Know Best

In 1983, I was four years old and lived on the left side of a lime-green duplex on the wrong side of the tracks in Kent, Ohio. Ronald Reagan was president, Michael Jackson was the biggest star in the world, and breakdancing was all the rage. Well, at least it was in my neighborhood. I often saw kids walking around with ripped-up pieces of cardboard boxes they had taken from the dumpster at the end of our street so they could bust a move wherever they were. I wasn't quite old enough to breakdance, but I was able to watch in awe and appreciate the amateur dancers from my front row seat on my red and blue Big Wheel bike.

Our duplex was on Silver Meadows Boulevard. Years later, I'd learn that our street also bore the local nickname "Silver Ghettos Boulevard." It wasn't exactly the nicest area, and people were always moving in and out—the U-Haul rental place at the end of the street did great business. I didn't know any better as a kid, and it didn't matter if we lived in the ghetto or Beverly Hills. Back then, that duplex was all Mom could afford—and if she hadn't been renting from my uncle, a successful accountant, she might not have been able to afford even that. Our house was a little over two miles from Kent State University, which flooded the city with college students during the spring and fall, and not far from Stow, the city where my grandmother lived. My grandfather died before I was born.

I was a fearless, easygoing, curious kid. Whenever I saw my neighbors outside, I would sprint out to join them and we would ride our bikes or play in the baseball field behind our house. Once, we found an enormous toad near our duplex and spent the entire afternoon chasing it. It didn't matter to me that Mom was always working, doing her best to raise three kids on a meager wage, or that I would get all my brother's hand-me-down clothes. Hot dogs, mac and cheese with pieces of breakfast sausage mixed in, and sugary cereal were our staples. I had my siblings, I had my grandma close by, and I had my neighborhood friends. Life was good.

Then, one late weekend afternoon in early October, I was playing with my favorite stuffed animal my grandmother gave me, Wicket from *Star Wars: Return of the Jedi*, in my room upstairs. I unexpectedly heard the doorbell and the sound of Mom opening the front door. A man's deep voice greeted her. *This is new*, I thought. It wasn't every day that someone showed up at our door. Curious, I raced downstairs to investigate.

When I arrived at the bottom of the stairs and didn't see anyone, I expanded my investigation. I turned the corner to head toward the dining room and on into the kitchen. As I entered the dining room, I froze in my tracks, my heart pounding. Standing before me was a towering figure. This giant stood well over six feet tall and was much larger than an average man. He sported a thick brown beard and a pair of bifocal glasses. My eyes traveled farther down to see he wore a green T-shirt and a beat-up brown Carhartt jacket. In his left hand he held a clear plastic bag containing a carton of chocolate marshmallow ice cream. His right hand was tucked into his jacket pocket.

Mom was in the kitchen, and my brother and sister were still playing upstairs. Alone with this giant stranger, I greeted him as any kid would greet such a large, intimidating man—with a punch on the leg. That's just the kind of kid I was—a punch to the leg was my way of saying, *Welcome!* I giggled, but for only a moment. The next thing I knew, a clenched fist the size of a softball was flying out of this man's pocket and toward my stomach. The impact felt like getting hit by a Mack truck going over seventy miles per hour. I keeled over in pain and gasped for breath, begging my lungs to start working again. Tears ran down my cheeks like a waterfall. I couldn't scream because I still couldn't breathe. It didn't matter anyway; nobody was coming to help me because nobody knew what had happened. I grabbed the corner of the daisy-patterned tablecloth that was on the dining room table, which looked more like a curtain, and used it as a tissue.

The towering man looked down at me and did not apologize. He didn't try to comfort me. He just stood there, watching. I assume he probably thought I'd gotten what I deserved for punching him in the leg for no reason. Afterward, it didn't take long for me to start to think that maybe I *had* deserved to get punched in the stomach.

I was only four years old, and this was my first meeting with my stepfather, Ben, or as my sister and I later referred to him, "Triple B": Big Bad Ben. This first meeting was pretty indicative of how our relationship would go.

By the time Triple B came along, it was me; my sister Kate who was a year-and-a-half younger than me; my brother, Kirk, who was two years older than me; and my twenty-eight-year-old mother. Mom had been divorced for less than a year, and she was desperately seeking a father for her three kids. Our biological father was completely out of the picture, aside from paying child support and sending obligatory cards on birthdays and holidays, and Mom didn't want him *in* the picture. Also, we didn't see our grandparents often on my father's side either and they died when I was very young. She didn't think he was a good father and later told me she never felt loved by him. But of all the men Mom could have met at the Kent State University Newman Center Singles' Night Mixer, she probably couldn't have picked a worse candidate to bring home than Triple B.

Like most kids, I was always looking for ways to have fun. At home, I was happy to play with Lego bricks, my He-Man action figure, or mess around with my siblings. Outside of the home, I wanted to make everyone laugh and smile. I was curious and made friends easily—when I got older, Mom liked to tell the story of how I used to just walk off at the grocery store and explore the aisles, introducing myself to strangers.

My life goal at that point was to be happy. And I couldn't understand why people were any other way. Until, that is, Triple B appeared in my life like a guest unwanted by everyone except Mom. It seemed to me that Triple B wasn't a happy person. In fact, I think he was the most miserable person I've ever met. He didn't laugh and didn't joke, unless it was the occasional racist or sexist joke, and he just complained about life and how everything and everyone was the worst. Traffic was his mortal enemy, every driver was out to ruin his day, and nobody could drive worth a lick, except him. He'd pull up to a light, trying to turn left, and announce that "every goddamn person and their mother" was out on the road that day, ruining his drive.

In hopes of lightening his mood and seeing a smile through his scruffy beard, I would often make jokes. "Why did the skeleton go to the movies alone?" I asked one day from the backseat of our early-eighties brown Chevy station wagon. "Because no-*body* would go with him," I said, providing the punch line to my own joke and cracking myself up in the process.

Triple B just glared at me in the rearview mirror through those dense bifocals of his with a look that said, *Stop talking. You're an idiot.* To him, everyone was terrible and an idiot. He was the only one justified in having an opinion.

Eventually, I lost some of my natural curiosity and rambunctiousness. Being around Triple B enough, I became more closed off, guarded. And I definitely wasn't fearless anymore.

A few months after Triple B came into our lives, early one morning, Mom woke us kids up and instructed us to put on our church clothes, even though we wouldn't be attending mass. Mine consisted of worn blue corduroy pants and a yellow polo shirt. We then piled into the station wagon and headed to the local courthouse so Mom could marry Triple B. Even though she was a devout Catholic and never missed a Sunday service, they weren't getting married in a church. I assume they didn't want to go through the trouble and expense of a real church wedding because it was the second bite at the apple trying to be husband and wife for both of them. My mother's first marriage had been annulled by the church—giving her the freedom to marry again. Only us kids attended the ceremony, and we sat on wooden pews in the gallery. Too young to understand what was going on, I joked with my brother about the silly man with a mustache wearing a black dress who was presiding over the ceremony. I quickly quieted down though when Mom glared at me, telling me to be good with only her eyes.

In addition to Mom's three kids, Triple B had two children of his own from his previous marriage: a six-year-old boy and a nine-year-old girl. They were going to live with us briefly before moving back with their mother. Creating this sudden large family forced Triple B and Mom to make some decisions in order to support us.

After high school, Triple B had joined the navy and spent most of his time deployed to Vietnam stationed on an aircraft carrier in the north Pacific. Together, Mom and Triple B determined that the best course of action was for Triple B to re-enlist in the navy. He became a machinist's mate second class and worked on the water pumps aboard ships. Being in the navy was not just a job; it was an adventure. At least, that was their slogan at the time. I didn't think the adventure applied to the servicemen's families, and I definitely didn't know that "adventure" really meant "nightmare."

Being a military family meant we had to move every four years. Our first stop on this navy "adventure" was Philadelphia. Philadelphia in the mid-eighties wasn't exactly the safest place. At least, it didn't seem that way to me. We lived in navy enlisted housing on base, which were basically run-down condominiums. The homes were just row upon row of the same connected units, all painted the same bland light yellow. The walls were as thin as paper, and I could repeat everything the neighbors discussed at their dinner table each night word for word. In turn, I'm sure the neighbors could hear the constant screaming and yelling on our side, especially when Triple B got home. I could easily smell the cigarette smoke or the aroma of meatloaf through the vents from neighbors four or five units down.

We also didn't do anything to make our home any better than it was, and you could never have mistaken Mom and Triple B for clean freaks. With seven people in the house at times, there was an endless amount of dirty dishes piled up in the sink, and it was always the kids' responsibility to clean them. I wouldn't be surprised to learn that Triple B actually had a phobia of warm water and dish soap, because he never once washed a dirty plate in over twenty-five years. However, he did seem to be an expert on how the dishes, pots, and pans should look when we were done washing them. I know this because he would inspect them, and if they were not up to his standards—and they rarely were—he would be furious, and we'd feel his anger in the form of a beating. Instead of cake for dessert, the kids were served lashings.

Because the kids were in charge of the dishes, it stood to reason that we would be expected to clean the rest of the house as well. Every child had assignments that rotated on a weekly basis. For example, my brother might be on dishes, my sister on dusting and vacuuming, and I would be on TC & F (table, counters, and floors). Because children were left in charge of cleaning, the drains were often clogged with week-old pasta, the refrigerator smelled, and tables were covered in dust more often than not. It wasn't rat infested or a total disaster area; it was just always cleaned as well as a pre-teen would clean.

What was a disaster, though, was the Philadelphia public school system. Due to all the horror stories I heard, I was under the assumption that if I even stepped into one of the schools, it would be the end of me. Think of all those heartwarming movies where the school's a wreck before the lead character, usually the principal, comes in and cleans it up, straightens all the kids out, and kicks out the riffraff. Those were the public schools in Philadelphia at the time. Graffiti covered the lockers, kids had to walk through a metal detector every day to get in, fights broke out on a regular basis, and kids cruised down the hallways on dirt bikes. (Okay, maybe not dirt bikes, but I know that image isn't too far off.)

Fortunately, I was able to dodge that bullet by attending a Catholic school called Holy Spirit. Mom insisted on it, in fact. Triple B wasn't crazy about paying for private school, but he wasn't crazy about anything. They were only able to afford it because of the child support Mom received and they got a break on the tuition since Triple B and Mom were sending so many kids there, and because of their meager income.

Mom was born and raised in the Cleveland area and although she was college educated, to help out with the finances, she took odd jobs depending on where we lived. She was a librarian in one place and a school lunch monitor in another. Mom would eventually become a histologist, which is a fancy word for the person who prepares tissue samples and puts them on slides for doctors to examine through a microscope.

Mom loved being a mother. She loved her children to death and would have done, almost, anything for them. Unfortunately, the one thing she wouldn't do is leave Triple B. The love she had for her children was also the reason Triple B was in our lives; she felt it was essential that my siblings and I have a father. In her spare time, she would bake, sew, and make quilts. She made quilts for all the kids' beds before they were ten. She made me feel like I was the best, and she loved all her kids that way. She even went so far as to make a shirt for me with "Kyle the Best" ironed on it. I was the only one who had such a shirt, which made me feel special. I wore that shirt constantly, and I believed I truly was the best kid ever born because of her.

I loved going to school because I loved being anywhere Triple B wasn't. I'd get up early in the morning, put on my uniform—black pants, a maroon sweater, and black shoes—head downstairs, and pour myself a bowl of Life cereal or whatever had been on sale that week at the grocery store. Then I'd head to the bus stop with my siblings. We all took the bus to and from school each day because by the time we left, Mom would already be at work, and of course there was no way Triple B would ever give us a ride.

Besides, even if it had been possible for them to take us to school, they wouldn't have. It was the kind of thing that didn't even occur to them: they got themselves to work, and we got ourselves to school. They didn't do it to teach us responsibility; it's something they just didn't care about.

Once at school, I would sing my heart out in choir and play four-square at recess. If I arrived early enough, I would go to the mass they held in the rectory next to the school. Scattered throughout the pews would be a few older women and a nun or two. When I was a kid, I wanted to be a priest when I grew up, so part of me thought I needed to be at mass all the time. However, thoughts of joining the priesthood quickly subsided once I hit puberty and found out just what celibacy meant.

Every winter, the school choir would travel to the local mall and perform a concert of Christmas carols. We all wore Santa Claus hats and belted out "Silent Night" to the crowds trying to get their last-minute shopping done as Sister Collette, my third-grade teacher, did her best impression of a conductor. Sister Collette was a stereotypical nun: a short older lady who always wore the full Roman Catholic habit who treated our mall performance as her opus.

Outside of home, it seemed like I had a "normal" childhood. I played soccer and baseball and I was the pitcher on my T-ball team. Mom came to every single one of my games and cheered me on, screaming, "Knock the cover off the ball!" Triple B never once attended any of my games.

At home, I lived in perpetual fear of upsetting Triple B. It was like constantly walking on eggshells. At dinner, if we put our elbows on the table while we were eating, he would stab us in the arm with his fork. Then there was the stick that Triple B nicknamed "Big Red."

Big Red was a piece of smooth wood about eighteen inches long and one and a half inches thick. At some point in its past, it had been spray-painted red. There was the outline of a dozen or so clothespins on the stick because it had been used as a background for one of our school projects. The stick was always conspicuously displayed in the house so all the children knew where it was. If we upset Triple B in any way, which didn't take much, the stick would come out.

One time when I was eight years old, I was watching TV with my brother and sister after dinner. I was tired and accidentally fell asleep on the chair with my head on the armrest. I was drooling a bit, and the drool got on the chair. Then I was rudely awoken by Triple B's grabbing my shirt and ripping me off the chair. I looked up and saw Triple B snarling in rage, yelling, "You're a fuckup! How many times have I told you not to do that?"

He threw me around like a rag doll until he felt certain that I was far enough away from the chair. I ended up being tossed against the wall in the hallway, knocking a framed picture of a lighthouse on the floor. "Don't fucking move," he told me as we walked into the other room.

I was shaking in fear and knew where this was heading. He came back with Big Red, and I started screaming for Mom to help me. She in turn was already yelling at him, begging him to stop. But nobody could stop him in that house. We all wished we could. That night, I went to bed with sores and bruises all over my legs from a few stick lashings.

We didn't know how to respond to Triple B, and during the worst years, none of us were able to stand up to him. We were all in shock, I think, from his violent introduction into our lives, and when he came for one of us, the rest of us could do nothing but let it happen. Sometimes if I saw my brother or sister getting hit, I would scream at Triple B to stop—but then he would tell me to stop crying, or else I'd be next.

None of us were spared—certainly not my brother, who, as the oldest, got into it with Triple B the most often and suffered his lashings the worst. We learned that the best thing to do was to stay away from him at all costs. When we couldn't do that, we all tried to please him and do what he said. There wasn't a moment of peace for any of us, as long as Triple B was around; the fear of being hit by Triple B was as bad as the actual beating if not worse.

Even when he wasn't physically abusing us, we would still suffer from having Triple B around. Sometimes he would make me and my siblings take showers down in the unfinished basement from a makeshift shower that sometimes had hot water and sometimes didn't—or we would just go without. He would also drag us out to the dumpster to collect aluminum cans to turn into cash. The three of us would jump in and pull out what we could so that he could collect the rewards while we got dirty.

Seeing the children she loved so much in pain hurt Mom dearly—I know this. Sometimes when I was getting beat by Triple B, my siblings would run to tell Mom, but then by the time she got there, it was too late. Not that it mattered, really; she had already witnessed our beatings with terror and tears in her eyes. She had asked him to stop, to no avail. Without the power to stop our pain, she would try to rationalize it, brushing it off as *boys being boy*s. Maybe she was able to convince herself that with me and my brother, it was a father-son moment that needed to happen. What more could she do? She didn't want another failed marriage on her hands. She rationalized that Triple B would change, or that things would get better. She thought that having a father figure in the house was necessary for raising a family, that having a physically and emotionally abusive father was better than having no father at all.

They say that prisoners and shipwreck survivors form a special relationship with one another, bonding over the shared experience of hardship. Well, that's what happened with me and my siblings. As Triple B imposed himself on all our lives, we formed a silent understanding: he was a terrible human, and we were going to have to rough this out, together and in our own separate ways. So we followed our mother's lead, normalizing the fear and abuse and moving on with our lives as best we could.

Looking back, I empathize with Mom. I understand this is her first time living life too. Neighbors and extended family members never saw (or didn't want to see) what was going on, but by the way Mom put on a show with them, pretending Triple B was a great dad, I could see how badly she wanted it to be true. Maybe if we would have all come together as a unified force, pleading for change, she might have been persuaded. But for whatever reason, we never did—maybe that helped her rationalize it, gave her the confidence to tell us it wasn't that bad, or the belief that the bad moments would be worth it in the end. All she ever wanted was a father for her children; instead, she got a miserable monster who just wanted to be by himself or around other like-minded miserable people.

Unfortunately, Triple B's anger and rage didn't stop with us kids, and he and Mom fought a lot. Neither of them knew how to be in a relationship; they just thought they had to be. We would be up in our rooms, playing with Micro Machines or Playmobil toys, pretending with tears in our eyes not to hear Triple B yelling at Mom downstairs, loud enough to shake the walls. One time, on our way home from a trip to the store, Mom and Triple B were screaming and yelling at each other in the car, and I couldn't stop crying because I wanted everyone to just be together and be happy. Triple B was threatening divorce, and as much as I was afraid of him, I didn't want him to hurt Mom's feelings.

As we arrived home and got out of the station wagon, Mom took my hand. I was in tears and asked her if everything was going to be okay. Triple B got out of the driver's-side door, still screaming at Mom. She asked him to tell me, a frightened, crying eight-year-old boy, that everything was going to be okay. He refused. He just walked into the house and told us to fuck off.

After that, I never looked forward to seeing him—ever. I prayed that he would just change, go away, or die. Every time he came home, I was afraid. All of us kids would hide in our rooms when Triple B got home and simply wait for Mom to call us to dinner. We were all constantly afraid of what would happen to us next. That fear, which may be worse than the physical abuse, lived with me as I grew up.

But it wasn't as easy as it should have been to avoid Triple B; from the start, Mom tried to force a relationship between us kids and him. She made us call him "Dad" and referred to him as our father, which only made me not want to call him either of those things. Plus, I already had a dad, albeit maybe not a great one. But I knew my biological father existed, and would see him once or twice a year.

I got the feeling that Triple B didn't care whether or not I called him "Dad"—he certainly never asked me to. He never did any of the standard fatherly things: he never took me to sports games, never played catch with me, never talked to me about girls, never taught me how to shave, never asked me how I was doing, never hugged me, never apologized to me for anything. There was no bonding of any kind. He called me names a lot—"loser" was his favorite. Our relationship was characterized by fear. I was afraid of him, and to him, I was just an annoyance. We had no connection.

Years later, as an adult, back in Ohio one afternoon, I was in the car with Triple B while he was running an errand, and we ended up taking a back road. As we drove down the twisting narrow road, we came upon a red covered bridge that had clearly been built in the late nineteenth century. As we passed it, Triple B pointed it out. "I proposed to my first wife on that bridge," he said.

"Oh yeah?" I responded, not knowing where he was going.

"It collapsed the next day," he continued. "I should have known from that that my marriage was going to fall apart."

That's odd, because when you walked into my house when I was only four, my whole life collapsed, too, I thought to myself.

This was the gist of most of his stories: he was always the victim of shitty situations. He told these stories to excuse his unacceptable behavior.

Triple B was pretty much the first and only male figure I'd ever had contact with, and so it took me a long time to realize that not all men were like him. All throughout my adolescence, I was somewhat afraid of every man I met, because I assumed they were all miserable people, too. It was like an epiphany when I discovered that half the world wasn't full of Triple Bs.

I would often read books or listen to music when I wanted to escape, but when I needed to get out of the house, I would stay the night over at a friend's house—they usually had the hottest toys and other things we didn't have at home, like cable TV. (I never had any friends over to my own house—I was too embarrassed and ashamed, and I always worried Triple B would hit me and my friend if we did something he didn't like.) In sixth grade, I remember going over to my friend Ted's house. Ted was a short, chubby redhead with freckles who lived on the nicer side of town. One day Ted showed me the new CD player that his dad had bought for him and the family. He played a CD of classical music and instructed me, as his dad must have instructed him, to listen for how it sounded differently than a cassette tape. It did sound different, I thought. I enjoyed it. At that time, I spent a lot of time in my room, alone, listening to the radio and cassette tapes—usually love songs. Later, I would copy the lyrics from memory to my notebook fantasizing about having that kind of love that was lacking in my life. But Triple B had never bought me anything, let alone a cassette player, and I would have never been allowed to play with an expensive toy or piece of technology without being yelled at.

It was nice, I thought, to be able to experience life as other people lived it. Like any other kid in my situation, I craved that sense of calm and joy—two caring parents who loved me just like the crooning singers on my cassette tapes loved the subjects of their songs, and who bought me nice things and let me enjoy them in a calm environment. But I didn't see that in the cards for me.

At first, I was confused and shocked when I encountered other kids' fathers who not only treated their kids with kindness but extended that kindness to their kids' friends. To me. Ted's dad was tall and skinny with thick black glasses—nothing like Triple B with his beard and bifocals, his massive hands that kept all us kids in fear. I was unable to digest this new information. My entire world was turned upside down, and it changed my way of thinking. *Maybe I don't have to live in fear for the rest of my life,* I thought. *Maybe I can choose to be happy.* Whatever I was going to be, I wanted to be the opposite of Triple B, and I was willing to do whatever it took to become that.

Right as we were moving away from Philadelphia, when I was around nine years old, my grandmother died in a car accident back in

Ohio. I still remember sitting in the station wagon with my family in a parking lot of the Navy Lodge. We were transitioning to Newport, Rhode Island and had a trailer attached to the back of the car. Mom could barely speak, and all of us kids were in shock. I started to cry and couldn't bring myself to drink my chocolate milk. I remember getting out to throw it out in the green dumpster in the parking lot and spilling some on me during the process. That, of course, threw Triple B into a rage.

"Stop crying before I give you something to cry about!" he yelled. I don't think he felt any sadness or empathy about Grandma; he was just upset that this event was going to delay our move. His yelling only made me cry worse.

In many ways, Grandma's death broke my mother. They had been very close, and Mom was never the same again. I was heartbroken, too. Before we moved to Philadelphia, we used to go over to Grandma's house to play games and do puzzles. She would cook us delicious dinners—not just the hot dogs or mac and cheese we were used to at our own house—and then we'd stuff ourselves with sweets. Grandma had the good stuff—Oreos, graham crackers, or homemade chocolate chip cookies that she brought out for us in her yellow Tupperware containers, decorated with happy designs of flowers and sunshine.

After dinner, when Mom and Grandma would sit and talk, my siblings and I would play Nintendo for hours in the living room, or we would go to her spare bedroom to build card castles or play war. One of the card sets was of a beautiful street scene—a bright moon and silhouettes of buildings on a green background. In my mind, when I thought of Grandma's house, I thought of that scene. It was somewhere we were all safe. She called me and my brother Lamb and my sister Boosit and would hold all three of us on her rocking chair singing: *Passing police man spied a little bum / Sitting on the sidewalk chewing pepsin gum / Said to him kindly, Won't you give me some? / Not on your tintype, said the little bum.* At the last line, she would always touch me on the nose. Afterward, we would all smell like cigarette smoke, but I never minded the smell. It reminded me of her. Like the card set, it made me feel warm and comfortable.

I have no idea what Grandma thought about Triple B, or what she knew about my mother's relationship with him, or how he treated us kids. But judging from what we all knew about Grandma, I would surmise that she knew Mom could have done better. I know she wouldn't have been pleased with the way he treated us or Mom. Maybe that's why Mom didn't bring him around very often. I have very little memory of Triple B being at my grandmother's house; for all I know, he might never have set foot onto the plush beige carpet of her living room, never sat on the chairs with embroidered flowers on them or Grandma's light peach colored couch, never grabbed a homemade cookie from her Tupperware containers. That's another reason why Grandma's house always felt so safe: There was nothing there to remind us of the terror we faced at home.

I wouldn't realize the full extent of Grandma's death—and its ripple effects—until many years later. It was an enormous loss, not just of the person but of a feeling of safety that all of us kids so badly needed. Without her, I didn't know what to do and had no one safe to turn to.

After her death, Triple B never once comforted me or even asked how I was coping. He didn't do that for Mom, either. When Mom fell apart at the funeral and actually fainted, Triple B just watched the whole thing from the back of the funeral parlor. His own wife fainted, and he didn't even take her in his arms and comfort her.

When we moved to Newport in 1989, there wasn't any navy housing available, so we were forced to rent a furnished home until space opened up on base. We moved into a place that was less than a mile from the ocean, but it was also run-down, and I had to share a bed with my brother. By this time Triple B's kids were gone; they were getting abused, too, and jumped at the opportunity to move back with their mother. I didn't blame them. To my knowledge, they didn't have much contact with Triple B as they grew up.

My siblings and I had to make new friends all over again, but at least we had a convenient escape from Triple B: Instead of hiding away in our rooms, we would go off to the woods near our house and build forts, or get lost playing hide and seek for hours.

While we were out there, we indulged in the one thing that Triple B hated most: humor. Once, when we were all out at the grocery store parking lot, my siblings and I were joking around and poking each other. In a rare moment of courage, we tried to loop Triple B into the fun by grabbing the skin on his elbow—but, thinking we were calling him fat, he blew up on us, and in moments we were sobbing. Out here, though, alone, we made fun of each other, trying on goofy accents and pretending to give each other life advice like we'd read in advice columns. Anything we could do to blow off steam, give ourselves a way to cope with Triple B's stifling negativity. We were never in any hurry to emerge from those woods and come back home because it meant coming back to Triple B.

And we had very good reason to dread coming home. In Newport, Triple B's beatings became more consistent. I don't know how my brother and sister were doing—we never talked about home when we were off playing in the woods—but I was starting to fall apart.

It was too stressful living in fear all of the time. I could see how our mom worried about money and about Triple B, and that only made me worried as well. Sometimes my siblings would disappear into their own private escapes—RC cars or scary movies for my brother, Barbies or making new friends for my sister—and I would be left alone with my fear.

Increasingly, Triple B turned his abuse toward Mom as well, screaming and yelling at her as if she were a child. Mom made dinner for the family every night, and she was a decent cook. One summer evening, I opened our screen door and came in from playing outside. I smelled the Italian sausage frying in the cast-iron skillet and the garlic bread baking in the oven, and I knew in an instant that we were having spaghetti for dinner—one of my favorites. The only problem was that Triple B wanted something different that evening. He wasn't in the mood for spaghetti, and he let Mom know about it. He had been blaming her for his weight gain lately, and he thought that the spaghetti in particular was contributing to the extra pounds he'd been putting on. Of course, he also refused to eat anything healthier or exercise.

As Mom dished out the sausage onto Triple B's plate, he swatted the spoon away with his hand and sent the sauce-covered meatball flying across the kitchen. He stood up, towering over Mom, and she backed up toward the open doorway leading to the basement stairs in fear. Spaghetti sauce dripped onto the floor from the spoon she still held.

"You want me to eat this shit and get fat?" he screamed in her face, almost shoving her down the stairs.

In tears, Mom grasped the side of the doorway with both hands as all us kids looked on from the dinner table without a word. We were terrified. Suddenly, Triple B backed off, sat back down, and started eating as if nothing had happened. We started eating, too—but I was crying inside.

I never actually witnessed him slap or punch Mom, but that doesn't mean that it didn't happen. But I did witness the emotional abuse—there's no question about that.

I now wonder why Mom didn't think she deserved better. Why didn't she think her kids deserved better? It must have been difficult for her to realize that while she was still holding out hope that Triple B would change or that things would get better—but they didn't. And instead of leaving, my mother kept pretending and rationalizing.

To deal with all the pain and uncertainty I felt at home, I badly needed an outlet beyond just sports. Back in Philadelphia, where I'd been an altar boy, the priests had been nice enough but they'd never given me the guidance I'd been seeking. My interest in the church had been less about a genuine interest in religion and more about a search for positive role models to help me deal with the emotions swirling inside me. Then, later on, I'd been in cub scouts. But Triple B was a former boy scout, and that was enough to turn me off of scouts before I got too far along. (I would eventually accumulate a long list of things I hated because of Triple B. The biggest one was trains—he was obsessed with trains and would drag the entire family out to watch them go by, or leave his model trains and magazines all over our house. It wasn't long at all before my siblings and I all hated trains.)

I started to interact more with other families, searching for the happiness I wasn't finding in my own home. I still remembered the night at my friend Ted's house—the CD player, the calm sense of peace and love in that home. I was constantly over at our neighbors' houses, looking to hang out, even if they didn't have kids. I was desperate to be around happy people.

Mom brought Triple B into our lives with the best of intentions, but the situation got away from her at some point. Mom showed me and my siblings love on a daily basis; she just wasn't equipped to deal with whatever Triple B was.

I assume Triple B just didn't know any better about how to raise a child. He didn't know how to be a father or how to love a kid. He was the way he was because of how he was raised: by an abusive father who disciplined with corporal punishment. Abuse has a way of trickling down from generation to generation. Still, I couldn't help but wonder what it would be like to have a real father. Mom always told me that my biological father was terrible because he wasn't around. I, in turn, always thought that not being around was much better than the emotional and physical abuse I received from Triple B.

Despite all of Triple B's shortcomings, there were a few silver linings to his being in our lives. He exposed me to camping. He didn't teach me how to start a fire or pitch a tent, but he took us to campsites on occasion. Living on the naval base, I was able to see all kinds of battleships. We would often travel around the country to visit old Civil War battle sites and see interesting historical places like Williamsburg, Virginia, or Gettysburg, Pennsylvania. Triple B would never explain why these sites were interesting or important—it was more for his curiosity—but at least I got to see them. Finally, an unintended consequence of Triple B's abuse was that it brought me closer to my brother and sister; being treated like crap by Triple B was something we all had in common.

After four years in Philadelphia and four years in Newport, Triple B retired from the navy, and we moved to his hometown of Cuyahoga Falls, Ohio. I was in the seventh grade at the time. The good news was that we were finally done moving around. The bad news was that I was getting old enough to really rebel and act out.

The physical abuse became less frequent as I got older. But instead of fading away into the dark recesses of my brain, the mind-twisting, all-out emotional abuse hurt more than I could have ever imagined—and emerged in ways I didn't even recognize. It was more than I could handle. I was about to realize that being raised on a steady dose of fear and abuse for years would have dangerous consequences now that I was coming of age.

CHAPTER 2

Drugs, Fighting, and Lawyering

In 1992, Tiger Woods became a PGA golfer, the Mafia crime boss John Gotti was sentenced to life in prison, and I was about to start my high school career.

"I'm not feeling anything," I said, frustrated, passing the homemade tinfoil pipe back to my across-the-street neighbor Michael, a kid who I'd thought was a Goody Two-shoes up until that point.

"I think it takes a few times," he said before he inhaled.

Neither of us knew what we were doing. The lights in the Saint Luke's Church parking lot just a few blocks away from the high school were not shining brightly enough to expose our nefarious activities in the dark corner, where we sat propped up against a chain-link fence.

The first day of high school was less than two weeks away, and I was attempting to get high off weed for the first time. Sure, I'd gotten a buzz before. I'd swigged whatever liquor was in Triple B's stash or chugged a beer from my friends' parents' house, or that someone swiped from the store. But I was always up for a new buzz.

The summer before high school, a group of us spent almost every day at a local nature park that was an extension of the Cuyahoga River valley. We'd go rafting or just get lost in the woods exploring. To add to our adventure, someone always managed to get their hands on some Marlboro cigarettes or Skoal chewing tobacco. Most of us being only fourteen or fifteen, we couldn't purchase those items on our own, so we stole them from the store or "borrowed" them from our parents. Once I took a hit of a cigarette or placed a wad of chew in my mouth and got that buzz, I wanted more of it. And just for a moment, I was able to escape and not have to think about my home life—or anything else, for that matter.

Before the drugs, when I was in eighth grade, I actually had goals of being a good student and attending a private high school. I even spent a "day in the life" of a student at a few of the Catholic high schools in the area where I attended classes and shadowed a student. It seemed to me that these kids had it all. They were smart, put together, and going places. They reminded me of my friend Ted. I wanted what they had; I was willing to bet they didn't have a Triple B at home.

I liked the idea of learning, but mostly I liked the idea that what I learned in school would allow me to achieve whatever I wanted and go wherever I wanted to go in life—preferably far from Triple B and Cuyahoga Falls. When I was younger, I wanted to be a secret service agent. I had watched the Zapruder film and thought I might like to be a heroic figure like the agent who jumped into the car after JFK was shot. Mostly, though, I think I liked the idea of saving someone in grave danger because I wanted so badly for someone to save me from Triple B. There was something romantic about that idea, being so important or so beloved that another person would risk their life for you.

As I got older, I felt open to any number of more sensible careers—I thought being a lawyer or teacher might suit me just fine—but I still felt that passion that had overtaken me back when I was daydreaming about becoming a secret service agent. I had a spark inside me. I don't know where it came from or how I kept it going through those early difficult years of childhood, but I had real dreams of making something of myself.

Private school seemed like my best shot to nurture that spark, escape my home life, and make it in the world. But our family just couldn't afford it. Plus, unlike in Philadelphia, where I'd attended a private school in lieu of braving the public school system, there were perfectly acceptable public schools in the area. With my brother already attending public high school and my sister probably going to do the same, sending me to a Catholic high school wouldn't have been fair to them. I'm not even sure why Mom let me go visit those private schools in the first place; she had to have known there was no chance I would be attending them.

I ended up at Cuyahoga Falls High School, which was only four blocks from my house. Ironically, for as badly as I wanted to get away from anything having to do with Triple B, I'd ended up at the same high school he had attended. Notwithstanding my introduction to drugs the summer before, I tried, briefly, to be a good student. Even though I didn't have the advantages of those private-school kids, I still felt that spark and wanted to give school my all. I even tried out, unsuccessfully, for the baseball team. I told myself that it was all politics—which, in some ways, it was—but deep down, I knew I wasn't good enough. I could have been better and practiced more and I could have refused to give up. But instead, I decided to move on. Although I ran track in middle school, I didn't even think about continuing in high school. It wouldn't have worked out anyway, because by the time track season came around, I was getting close to smoking a half a pack of cigarettes a day. My goals of being a good student and playing sports were quickly eclipsed by three other things: drugs, girls, and my "friends."

I've never had a problem making friends. It's choosing the right friends that has always been my issue. The friends I had in high school were just an extension of how I felt about myself at the time. They represented what I thought friends were supposed to be; we communicated by constantly putting each other down and making fun of each other. Just like I didn't know what a father was supposed to act like, I didn't know what real friends were supposed to act like. This only compounded my rebelling and acting out. I had nobody I could confide in or to really support me. If I was anxious about a test, my friends called me a loser; if I liked a girl, they would tell her that I wasn't a good guy. I would have been better off asking a stranger for help or advice. They would ditch me to go to parties or take me with them to a party and then leave without telling me. In turn, I'd do the same to them. I continued to be friends with them because I didn't know any better and because I didn't think I had much of an option.

I had one friend named Jerry who treated me like shit. But I looked up to him because he was older, got girls, and made money. Sometimes when we hung out, he would take me to scary drug houses even though I said I didn't want to go, then leave me there and say he'd be back. Instead, he'd go meet up with a girl and never come back to pick me up. If I had money and he needed it, he'd take it from me. If he got in trouble with his family, he'd blame it on me. I didn't just accept this type of behavior—I internalized it and adopted it in my other friendships.

I wasn't just an asshole; after an entire childhood of being bullied by a bigger, stronger, crueler man, I became a bully myself. Because my "friends" and I treated each other like crap, I treated the rest of the world like crap, too. I'd put everyone down every chance I got. I thought I was somehow superior to people who looked weird or had their own unique personality. I just needed the smallest reason to call people out. I had no idea what kind of impact I was having on others or how hurtful I was being. Inside I was just jealous because they seemed happy with who they were and weren't afraid to express it. I had no basis for anything I was telling others. I just said it. It got to the point where I would pick fights with anyone—so long as I knew I could win. They didn't have to do anything to me; I just wanted to do something to them.

There was a girl I went to high school with; she had purple hair and a nose ring—she was expressing herself and was confident in who she was and didn't care what people thought. She was a perfect target for my jealous, insecure high school self. One day I was calling her names like "freak," getting a good laugh from friends. I didn't think much of it that day, but I guess she did. That week, I was sitting in the cafeteria, enjoying my lunch when all of a sudden I felt this hot, burning liquid on my scalp. The purple-haired girl had poured hot soup on my head causing first degree burns. I jumped up and ran to the nurse's office. The police were called, as is the case when any student is injured by another student. As I was in the nurse's office the police asked if I wanted to press charges. Although I was angry and upset, there was no way I wanted to have her arrested. I told them "no". I felt so much compassion for that girl at the moment and immediately regretted my name-calling. It's not that I didn't think I deserved boiling, hot soup dumped on my head—which I probably did. But I understood why she was upset. I could relate to her. I knew what it was like to have someone be mean and abusive to you for no reason, just for being yourself. She didn't deserve that and I didn't want to be like that.

I didn't fare much better in my relationships with girlfriends. If I was dating one girl, Jerry or one of my other friends would tell me how ugly she was, or say that she was no good for me. When I stopped seeing her, one of them would be dating her the next week. Even without my friends stepping in, though, I was lost when it came to girls. I had no idea how real relationships worked, so girls came and went as often as the seasons changed. It was mainly my fault. If they got too emotionally close, I knew it was time to move on because I was so afraid of feeling something and getting hurt. Or I would seek out and date girls who had their own set of problems. One of my first serious girlfriends, for example, had family issues. Her father was abusive, and her mother was an alcoholic. She was on Ritalin and would come to school drunk or high. I guess I was attracted to someone else who had issues like I did and would sneak off in the middle of the night to meet her. But it didn't last long, and I later learned that she cheated on me. She eventually flunked out of high school and never came back. No judgment there—my own issues were only just beginning.

Most troubling of them all was my drug use, which progressed quickly. I wanted the buzz, and all the "cool" kids were doing drugs— at least, that's what I thought the cool kids were doing. Whether it be inhaling nitrous oxide, smoking pot, or dropping acid, I wanted to do it. Although I was a regular weed smoker and beer drinker, the drug that I believe had the most severe consequences for me was the hallucinogen LSD—acid.

At the time, acid came in doses, called "hits," on little pieces of paper about the size of a popcorn kernel. I probably took a few hundred hits of acid over the course of my illustrious high school career. As with most drugs, the first time I took acid, I thought it was amazing. My friends and I would hang out at a local skateboarding spot—behind a dance studio that had a nice waxed up curb to do nose slides and grinds on. We seemed to do drugs more than actually skateboard. The euphoric feeling of doing acid was quite different from the buzz I got with weed or alcohol. It was like a whole new world had been opened up to me. I started noticing things I'd never noticed before: colors were brighter, people seemed happier, and I even thought I was happier, if only for a moment. It was like the blinders had been pulled from my eyes, and I could finally really see the world for the first time. I was now "awake" and looked at the world differently. I didn't really have any hallucinations—probably because we weren't getting the cream of the crop of acid in northeast Ohio—I just saw lots of trails of things that moved. If I waved my hand in front of my face, it was like watching a cartoon with the animation not quite sped all the way up, so there were trails behind it.

Although I thought I was getting a closer connection to the world and to my true self, I was actually going in the opposite direction. I was getting farther and farther from what I was seeking and what the world was actually like. And, as with any drug, the more acid I did, the more I needed to take to get the same feeling I'd had the first time.

Eventually, after taking acid too much, I had a "bad trip." My friend Mitch and I were alone in the living room of my house. At first, I was just a little bit paranoid. But then that paranoia grew into fear, which then turned into me freaking out and becoming hysterical. I had a million thoughts racing through my mind at once, and all of them were bad. I thought people were out to get me, that I was going to die, or that I was going completely mad. While I was on this bad trip, I was certain I was going to be in this state forever and that was the scariest part of all. I thought I was going crazy, and I didn't know what to do. At some point I stripped down to my boxers and curled into the fetal position, begging Mitch to take me to the hospital. That seemed like the only solution at the time. He refused, probably because he was tripping, too. We were lucky that Triple B wasn't home; I assume he would have called the cops immediately.

I woke up the next morning alone in my bedroom, relieved to have all my faculties still intact. The bad trip was one of the worst things I've ever felt or experienced in my life. I was so impacted by it that I vowed I would never do acid again—which was one of many lies I told myself.

Then, in a blink of an eye, freshman year was over.

During my sophomore year, I decided to ditch my old friends and hang out with even worse ones. Luke the drug dealer seemed like the best option. He had long blond hair, wore Alice in Chains and Primus T-shirts, and already had a reputation for being a druggie. Luke treated me like crap, but he also kept me high, so I took it. With Luke, I upped the ante and started doing cocaine. I don't even remember the first time I did coke, but I know I liked it a lot and always wanted more. And it didn't stop with cocaine. A few times, we put the crystallized form of cocaine—crack—on weed, lit a match, and smoked it. For some reason, that's where I decided to draw the line with drugs. I knew that getting into this realm of drug use was a whole other level and that I was going overboard and taking this drug thing a bit too far.

Although Luke was not the best person to hang out with, he did leave me with a valuable skill: entrepreneurship. The jobs I, briefly, had at McDonald's and Taco Bell weren't cutting it—not for a kid who needed to get high every day. The free food was great, but I knew it was possible to make so much more without flipping burgers or slinging tacos. And thanks to my relationship with Luke, I knew who to go to in order to get larger quantities of drugs to distribute.

I started out small, just getting an ounce of weed at a time and breaking it up into eighths and quarters. I could buy an ounce of crap weed for around $160. I'd break that ounce up into eight separate bags, sell those bags for $30 each, and make $240. That's quite a profit margin, especially for a sixteen-year-old. I often kept one of those bags for myself and sold the rest.

I would sell across the street from school, or anywhere else kids wanted to meet us. I had a pager back then and would get notified of a sale and then tell them to meet us at my friend's house on Third Street, or I'd go to them. Sometimes Luke and I would hang out at a parking lot down on Front Street by the Cuyahoga River, skateboarding and waiting for buyers to meet us there. It was easy because there was a pay phone there, and the location was hidden under a bridge—we'd call and say, *Come down to Front Street, under the bridge.* We sold to kids in NBA Starter jackets, kids with blue hair and wallet chains, jocks from the football team, kids I knew, and kids I'd never seen before in my life.

One ounce turned into two ounces, which turned into half pounds of weed, which I could easily sell in a week. Going out to dinner with my friends became an odd experience because I would have over $500 cash on me while my other friends were struggling to pay for their slice of pizza. It felt good—not just to make money but to have other kids treating me with respect (only because they wanted something from me, sure, but still). I could tell that the jocks wanted nothing to do with me and thought they were better than me—but they had nowhere else to go. There was power in that, too.

I soon discovered that selling acid was much more lucrative than selling pot, and it also wasn't as involved and messy. I could get a sheet of acid with one hundred hits on it for around $200 and sell those for five bucks apiece—sometimes ten bucks, depending on who I was selling to. Do the math. I was rolling in cash for a kid my age at the time. I quickly gained a name for myself in high school as the go-to drug dealer. I learned how to hide hits of acid in my pen to sell during class. I would get paged in geometry to meet someone in the third-floor bathroom for a quick sale. This was essentially my life when I was sixteen.

My grades started to drop, not like they had far to fall in the first place. What frustrated me the most, though, was how everyone else my age seemed to be able to handle doing drugs and still function at a normal level. It seemed like I was the only one who couldn't handle their effects. Looking back, I see now just how close I was to the edge of the cliff, hanging on for dear life. I didn't realize that not everyone came from the same kind of home life I did. They were sobering up for family dinners and game nights, dodging inquiries from concerned parents. They weren't looking for excuses to stay away from home, or searching for anything that might distract them from what awaited them there.

When I wasn't selling drugs or getting into fights at school, I was at my friend's place on Third Street becoming an expert in three things: doing drugs, playing cards, and playing foosball. My buddy's house was a safe place for all of us degenerates. I suppose it was at least better than running around on the streets. We didn't actually hang out in the house, but rather a remodeled garage behind the house where local bands practiced. We had to enter through the main door on the side because the garage door didn't open and had all kinds of garbage and old furniture stacked up in front of it anyway—chairs, couches, plastic pools. Inside wasn't much cleaner.

There were adults around, but they weren't doing much of

the parenting that they should have been doing. My friend's dad saw himself as a manager of sorts, scouting the local bands who were always playing there, but really, he just liked getting high and listening to rock music. It was a strange situation: He and my friend's mom would do his homework for him and let him stay out as long as he liked. The kids had bedrooms in their house, but the parents slept on the living room floor. They had transient friends who would come and go, staying for days or weeks in the basement or in the garage. None of it was normal, but I didn't think twice about it back then. None of us did.

It was the perfect scenario: I was able to sell and do drugs as much as I wanted there. Plus, it was only a mile or so from my house, so I had easy access to it. It didn't matter who was there, and I didn't have to call beforehand—the door was always unlocked, so I would just show up and hang out with whoever was present. Somebody was always there and ready to get their buzz on. We'd walk through the drums and speakers scattered across the garage, fire up the wood stove in the back that we fed with anything that burned to keep the place warm, then put the chairs in a circle around the stove and get high. We would play euchre, spades, poker, gin rummy, king's corner. If none of my friends were there, I would get high with my friend's dad or have him and his friends buy me malt liquor. If we liked the bands practicing, we would hang out with them or sell them drugs. If we didn't, we would go out back behind the garage and get high in the old camping trailer that was permanently parked there. It was the perfect escape. It was so close to my house; on some nights, I would wait until Mom and Triple B fell asleep and then sneak back out and stay up all night.

Although Triple B's physical abuse was becoming less frequent as I got older, the emotional and verbal abuse was increasing. Triple B didn't shy away from calling me degrading names. He said it to my siblings, too, but for whatever reason, they stayed on the straight and narrow. Maybe they were stronger than me, less sensitive, better able to cope with the abuse. Maybe they were smarter and knew that getting good grades would be the best way to escape Triple B's wrath—and, eventually, his house. But the more abuse I had to deal with, the more I looked for an easy out, and my drug use soon spiraled out of control.

At school, it seemed like I had a standing appointment with the principal every week because I was in her office so often. Her name was Ms. Koch, and she was a short lady in her late forties who had a penchant for pastel pantsuits. I never got the sense that Ms. Koch, or anyone in the administration, cared too much about my well-being. She never tried to help me or give me the tools to change. I was more of a nuisance she had to deal with. No one ever asked if my home life was okay or what was bothering me. I'm not sure whether I would have told them but I was definitely never given the chance to find out. It was like I was a lost cause to them. To be fair, that's what I felt like.

I would be sitting in class, daydreaming, when a student would walk in with a blue slip of paper and hand it to the teacher. I knew exactly what that meant and so did everyone else: I was being summoned yet again. And there was only one reason why I would be called to Ms. Koch's office: I was getting suspended again. I was suspended at least a dozen times during my high school tenure, generally for getting into fights and for skipping school, the punishment for which was getting kicked out of school for a few days. It seemed like a great trade-off to me.

The worst part about suspensions, the reason I hated going to the principal's office so much, was that they called Mom. It ate me up inside knowing she was going to get a call at work. My brother and sister never got suspended, and they both got decent grades at worst. But I was putting Mom through hell. I knew that Mom was at her wit's end, never knowing when she was going to get "the call" at work, and I hated it, but I also didn't do anything about it and didn't know what to do about it. At the time, I cared more about my friends, girls, and doing drugs.

I don't think my suspensions did much to change Triple B's opinions of me. One day I was skipping school with my girlfriend and we were hanging out at my house. During the day my house was usually empty because Mom and Triple B were at work. However, on this particular day Triple B came home for lunch. As I heard him pull into the driveway I freaked out—we didn't have time to escape. I told my girlfriend to go hide upstairs in my room—I was going to have to confront Triple B on my own. As he walked in the back door that led to the kitchen I was in there waiting for him. He looked at me a little startled. With my voice shaking, I just started telling him how I didn't feel good and that's why I was home. He didn't say anything. He moved past me giving me a shove, opened the refrigerator and grabbed a brown bag out, then walked toward the back door. Right before he opened the door, he turned to me and said, "you're a fucking worthless loser," and slammed the door shut and left. I knew better than to be around when he got back home that day.

Although I was always getting into fights, I hated fighting and was always scared. I did it because I wanted people to like me, to think that I was cool. I thought I had something to prove. I wanted people to think I was a badass fighter, but I really wasn't. I was a coward.

The fight that broke the camel's back was with a kid we called

Buddy. I was making fun of him—I made fun of everyone because I thought that's what I was good at. People laughed, so I kept it up. Buddy wore a cowboy hat and had ripped-up jeans, and that was enough for me.

At lunch one day, I called him a hillbilly and he didn't take too kindly to that. Buddy came at me in a fury, swinging and screaming, and we started fighting in the hallway outside the cafeteria. Because my druggie friends didn't care about getting suspended either, they jumped in to help, and I would not have made fun of Buddy if my friends weren't close by. They knew I couldn't have taken him by myself; he was a lot bigger than me or my friends, over six feet tall with an athletic build. Several of us ended up putting Buddy in the hospital with a busted lip, two black eyes, and a bruised ego. Not only did I get expelled from school, I was also arrested. It should have been a major wake-up call for me—Buddy left in an ambulance, and I was in handcuffs. And for what? Because I had to be a bully? I spent the rest of that year mowing lawns for a landscaping company and doing community service.

The fighting didn't stop just because I was out of school, though. One day, my friends and I were driving down the street when we saw a few kids who we thought were different in some way—greasy hair and dirty clothes—so we gave them the middle finger and yelled at them. To our surprise, they flipped us off right back. Little did they know that we had weapons with us in the form of a few collapsible batons, similar to what the police carry. These weapons gave us the confidence we needed to go after them. We quickly parked the car, jumped out, and chased down one of these kids through various backyards and beat him up. We didn't use the batons on him, though. We didn't need to, as we had him outnumbered.

When we got back to the car, we were greeted by the police. It seemed a concerned neighbor had witnessed the scuffle and made a call. I was arrested, again, and charged with felonious assault because we had weapons with us, which meant I faced significant time in juvenile detention if the charge stuck. This time, I was in major trouble. Not only was I facing a serious charge, but my mother had to hire a lawyer. To make matters worse, Mom ended up getting sued by the parents of the kid we beat up. Luckily for me, my lawyer was able to get the felony charge reduced to a simple assault, and I was spared a sentence in juvenile detention. The kid's parents got a small monetary compensation. Mom was scared for me and was doing anything she could to help me. However, Triple B was not happy about my arrest and getting sued. He told Mom that a lawyer was a waste of money and I was getting what I deserved. Maybe he was right, but Mom felt like she had to do something if she was able.

Again, that should have been the thing that made me turn my life around. Afterward, I felt like a complete idiot—I'd gotten swept up in the moment, wanting to look cool for my friends. Though I never thought of myself as a violent person, I'd gotten a world-class lesson in violence from Triple B. I didn't really want to hurt anyone—I was bawling just before I was arrested—but fighting was the only way I knew how to make a statement about my life. I was angry, I didn't have an outlet, and I needed to take that anger out on someone. It wasn't who I was, or who I wanted to be. But I was scared, and that fear made others fear me, too.

Still, that wasn't the end of my fighting or getting arrested. I was arrested for trespassing, having an open container of alcohol in public, disorderly conduct, and disturbing the peace, all before I was eighteen. And then there were all the other things I never got caught doing, like breaking into cars and houses and shoplifting. It was clear to me—and it should have been clear to just about anyone who knew me—that I was out of control. But I couldn't stop myself from spiraling, and it was starting to seem as if no one else could either.

As I was heading back to school for a second shot at my junior year, I was starting to feel helpless. I had nobody to turn to or confide in. To the school administration, I was just another nuisance. At the police station, I was just another juvenile delinquent. I couldn't talk to Mom because she was so defensive about the father she had chosen for us that she couldn't see what was really going on and why I was acting out so much.

Luckily, a small miracle happened that year. The school caught on that I didn't mind getting suspended, so they put me in in-school suspension. In-school suspension is where I had to spend the whole day in a classroom with other troubled students. We couldn't talk or sleep, and we were only allowed two bathroom breaks a day, which had to be supervised by a teacher. I had to bring a bagged lunch, and my teachers sent my homework to me from my classes. Having to spend so much time in there was my saving grace, because in that room, without distractions, I couldn't get into any trouble.

It was there that I met Mr. Brady, the in-school-suspension teacher, who started to get to know me over the course of the year. Mr. Brady was a young teacher with an athletic build and a clean-shaven baby face—he must have been in his mid-twenties at the time. He wore ties with short sleeve button-ups and wasn't afraid to joke around with me. If I had questions about school work, he would assist me. He actually took the time to help me understand that I could achieve so much more if only I applied myself. He told me that I was smart and had a lot going for me. He was the first male authority figure to ever tell me that he believed in me and that I could be better. It blew my mind that not all adult men were miserable jerks who I needed to fear. I had already developed quite the reputation, not just among my peers but also among my teachers. Mr. Brady, though, never treated me like a delinquent, even though I acted like one.

There was also Mr. Bishop, the biology teacher. He was an older man, maybe in his sixties, slim with glasses and a salt-and-pepper goatee. One day he caught me smoking weed in the bathroom with my friends. I thought he was going to take me to the principal's office when he dragged me out of there. Instead, something quite different happened.

"Kyle, the guys you're hanging around with don't care about you," he said. "They don't want the best for you. I promise you, when you have real friends in your life, you will figure it out right away because they will make you feel good about yourself." I listened to him with my head down, leaning up against the wall of his classroom, knowing in my heart he was speaking the truth.

These talks with Mr. Brady and Mr. Bishop planted a seed in my mind. In many ways, it seemed as if I had been waiting for a male role model to tell me what they told me. I hadn't gotten it from Triple B or from the priests in Philly. My friends' fathers had been kind to me, but they weren't my father. Once, Mom asked my uncle to have a talk with me when I was on the verge of flunking out of high school the first time, but he put all the blame on me, telling me that I should be much better than I was. It fell flat, not only because he didn't understand the severity of my situation but because he made no attempt to understand me, put himself in my shoes, or try to empower me. These men, Mr. Brady and Mr. Bishop, made me look at who I was and what I wanted out of life. And when I completed that internal audit, I didn't like what I saw.

One day shortly after both of these talks, when I wasn't in in-school suspension anymore, I was sitting in my behavioral science class, staring out the window. Mr. Anderson was passing back a test we had taken the week before. Written at the top of my paper was a large red "F." This wasn't surprising or unusual, except this time, I felt different about it. I knew I could have passed, and it really frustrated me. I felt as if I had no control over my life, and I knew it was time to make a change. I got up and left class immediately. I found my friend Brad, who I knew would leave school with me, and asked him to drive me to drug rehab. I didn't know if it was the right thing to do, or if it would save me. All I knew was that I needed to do something, anything, to stop the madness and chaos swirling around me.

The rehab center I went to was for juveniles only, and it was in a fully functioning hospital in Barberton, Ohio—the very hospital where my mother worked. Once I arrived, I realized that I couldn't just turn myself in. As a minor, I needed to be admitted by court order or have a parent sign me in. When I first arrived, they had no idea what I was doing—I learned that I was actually their first patient to try and voluntarily enter rehab without a parent or guardian. They paged Mom down so that she could sign me in and I was admitted.

I'll never forget Mom's face in that moment. I expected surprise or shame or disgust, or maybe even anger. Instead, there was a sense of relief that seemed to sweep across her face when she realized I was there. She seemed to immediately understand that I needed help—that I probably had for some time—and she knew exactly where to go and what to do. I remembered her telling me, months before, "Tell me what to do to help, or I don't know how to help." I didn't know either. But now rehab was my answer—and it seemed that it was the answer she'd been searching for as well. It was possible, I later realized, that she had been dropping hints about the rehab center at her hospital—that must have been how I knew it was an option.

Drug rehabilitation was one of the most amazing experiences I've ever had. I felt so safe there. Nobody could hurt me, and I couldn't hurt myself by doing drugs. We weren't allowed to leave our wing of the hospital, where we had our own bedrooms, a cafeteria, and a communal room where we would all talk, play games, and have group therapy. There was a strict schedule, which I liked. I knew when it was time to eat and what activities we were doing. I also liked being around a bunch of other people my age who had also screwed up their lives.

Occasionally we would leave our hospital wing, piling into a beat-up old cargo van to attend bleak AA meetings in the middle of the day, listening to retirees share their stories about being drunk. The more I heard, the more I knew this wasn't where I belonged. They would tell stories of hiding their alcohol use from their family or sleeping in a ditch after drinking all night and being woken up by a street cleaner. Or passing out in their car driving home and being woken in a cornfield by a cop. I realized that I had an addictive personality and definitely had issues doing things in moderation. I wasn't necessarily addicted to drugs, but I definitely had an unhealthy relationship with drugs and alcohol.

Triple B never came to see me, which I preferred. To him, my going to drug rehab was just more of an affirmation that I was a worthless loser. When Mom visited me, I had her stop at the store first and bring me cigarettes—a humiliating task for her, I later realized, to need to supply her teenage son with nicotine at the drug treatment center.

But the humiliation didn't end there. As part of the healing process, we were supposed to tell the family members who visited us *every* drug we had ever done. This was the worst part of rehab for me; I was embarrassed and didn't want to hurt Mom any more than I already had. But they said it was necessary for my recovery, so I wrote it all down on a piece of paper and gave it to Mom. I knew she didn't know the extent of my drug use and I could see the disappointment written all over her face as she read it. At least my being in rehab meant that she knew I was in a safe place and getting help.

After a month or so in rehab, when the insurance ran out, I graduated to outpatient status. This was where I was supposed to stick with the program on the outside. I kept it up for a few weeks—Mom wanted me to, and I did, too. Even if I wasn't an alcoholic, I needed something to help stop me from the path I was on and reset me for the next chapter of my life. If I was going to make something of myself, I would have to focus now that I was back outside the safe environment of rehab. Eventually, though, I headed back over to the garage on Third Street. A girl I liked was over there, and she was drinking. Someone handed me a forty-ounce bottle of Colt 45 Double Malt, which I immediately took a swig of. And just like that, I was back.

People knew me because of the crazy things I did, like selling drugs, getting in fights, and running the "trash can clan," a nickname kids in school gave me and my group of friends because we congregated around, well, a garbage receptacle. As much as I wanted to stay clean, in my mind, if I didn't have those things, I was insignificant. I had spent so much time seeking and being denied approval from Triple B as a child; as a teenager, I was just as scared of not having any friends, not being cool. At one point, I actually told my rehab counselor that if I followed all their rules, I would be a loser. I believed it so much that it scared the hell out of me. In high school—or at least when I was in high school—an outcast is the worst thing a kid can be. Luckily—or unluckily—for me, my stint in rehab gave me a new sort of street cred with my peers. From their point of view, I had just gone on a cool vacation, and they wanted to hear all about it.

Because of my stint in rehab I repeated my junior year, mostly without incident. But strangely, for as much fighting as I had done in my previous five years of high school, it was a fake fight during my senior year was the most memorable and scary—and changed the course of my life more than any of the others.

There was a kid a little bit older than me who didn't go to our high school but would hang out across the street from school, where everyone stood and smoked cigarettes after class let out. This was where I could usually be found after school. I often made fun of this kid to others, but my mistake was making fun of him to his girlfriend, who was in one of my classes. She told him about it, so after school on this day, I realized this kid was looking for me.

When school let out, I went across the street like I usually did. As I walked past the crowds of smokers trying to find my friends, I could hear a voice screaming: "Who is Kyle Robinson? Where is Kyle Robinson?" I looked over and saw him with raging fury in his eyes and saliva flying out of his mouth. He easily had six inches and fifty pounds on me. I tried to keep my head down and walk past him as fast as I could; my heart was racing and I was scared shitless. But everyone started pointing me out to him. My friends were nowhere to be found, and to make matters even worse, I wasn't a minor anymore, so if I got arrested, I'd be in serious trouble, and real jail was something I desperately wanted to avoid. I was fucked.

The kid spotted me and made his way toward me, ready to pound me into the ground. I tried to back away from him, even running around in circles trying to avoid him, telling him I didn't want to fight. A crowd gathered around us screaming "fight" as I dodged him. Eventually a police officer came by to break things up, arresting us both before a punch was even thrown. My charges, I would soon learn, were disorderly conduct, disturbing the peace, and assault. There was no more in-school suspension; now I was facing jail time.

When my day in court came along, my mother accompanied me. I pled not guilty and represented myself because Mom wouldn't get me an attorney. I had explained to her that I hadn't done anything wrong, but I don't think she believed me. I was telling the truth this time, but even though I had done nothing criminally wrong, I knew I had caused the fight through my past behavior—and that it was my past behavior, too, that would be working against me as I argued my case.

The day of the trial, I sat at the defense table by myself, wearing my shirt and tie. I liked being the center of attention, normally—but not this way. Mom sat behind me. (Triple B was, of course, absent.) The prosecutor sat at the table to my left, the judge on the bench in front of us. Otherwise the court was mostly empty. I knew all of this was serious—there was a real judge in a robe, a real prosecutor, even a bailiff, all of them here for me. The only time I'd seen a courtroom was on TV, but this didn't feel at all like TV, especially not with my fate on the line.

Still, I knew I was in the right. I was nervous, but I wasn't afraid—

until, that is, I saw the arresting officer on the witness stand. I could feel myself starting to sweat as I thought about all the times I'd run into authority figures over the last few years. This time, though, it felt different. I was doing it on their own terms, in the correct way. The way that wouldn't get me in trouble—if only they would believe me.

The trial began, and the prosecutor started asking the officer questions. "Do you see the person who was involved in the altercation?"

"Yes," the officer said, pointing at me.

After the prosecutor asked a few more questions, the judge asked if I wanted to ask the officer any questions. *Hell yeah!* I thought. It was clear to me, based on the crowd that had gathered around me at the "fight," and based on the officer's questions, that he had no idea what had happened. I was nervous almost to the point of tears as I prepared to ask my questions. It was very intimidating, and I had no idea what I was doing. But I had practiced, at least a little bit, writing down what had happened and repeating the story to myself over and over again. I had to be convincing; not even Mom believed me.

I cleared my throat and pushed ahead.

"Where were you when you first saw this altercation?" I asked, my voice shaking.

"I was sitting in my police cruiser," the officer replied confidently.

"And how far away was your police cruiser from the disturbance?"

"About seventy-five yards."

"Was there a crowd of people around me and the other individual you arrested?"

"Yes, about one hundred or so kids."

"So you can say for certain that while you were sitting in your police cruiser seventy-five yards away, you could see clearly through a crowd of one hundred kids that I was involved in some sort of altercation?" I pushed back.

I looked up at the judge. Maybe I was crazy, but he didn't look skeptical or angry. He was being patient, giving me the opportunity to present my case, and he looked supportive, almost like he was telling me, *You can do this, I believe in you.*

"Well, not exactly," the officer admitted.

"So you never actually saw me assault anyone?"

"No," he finally answered.

That was all the judge had to hear. The case was dismissed, and the charges were dropped. The entire trial had lasted less than a half hour.

It was one of the most amazing moments of my life. The police officer may not have been lying; with my record, too, he had every reason to believe I had been involved in another fight. Nor did it matter that I wasn't truly innocent, that I had created the situation for myself by making fun of someone who hadn't deserved it. To me, still, it was a miracle: a nineteen-year-old defending himself against almost insurmountable odds. It felt like I had escaped, however narrowly, a path that was going to lead me to a life in and out of jail, or worse. And if I could do that, what else was I capable of? I thought of Mr. Brady, the seed of belief he'd planted in my mind: that I was smart, I was capable, I wasn't destined to be the fuck-up that Triple B believed me to be. At some point, I had started to believe him—and started to believe in myself.

There was something else that was sparked in me, as well. All I knew about lawyers before that pivotal moment was that they were rich, smart people. All the lawyers I'd ever met had looked down on me as a lost cause, even the one we hired to represent me as a juvenile. I'd always thought it would be nice to make a lot of money but that path wasn't open to me—both because of my past and because of what it would take to get a law degree. Hell, I still wasn't sure whether I was going to graduate high school.

But after that case, after I'd successfully defended myself, I started thinking about things differently. I knew now that I could work within the legal system and be successful. I knew that the authorities weren't always right—that even humans in suits could make mistakes, or lie for their own advantage. Everyone in that room, other than Mom, had wanted to see me arrested, hoping I'd go away like most people who are arrested. But I'd refused to accept the narrative they'd scripted for me, and they didn't like it. It was a small thing, really, a single moment in court, but I was really starting to believe the messaging I'd received from Mr. Brady and Mr. Bishop: I was smart enough to be successful in life. And once the adrenaline of that situation started to wear off, I started thinking about how cool it might be to be on the other side of the law some day. To be around those high stakes situations—guilty or not guilty, prison or freedom—without yourself being in jeopardy. It felt to me like a safe position—and I wanted nothing more than to be in a safe position.

By my senior year, I had a new principal named Mrs. Horner. She was one of the better faculty members, and knew me well enough to understand that I would get into trouble if I spent time going to regular classes hanging around my "friends." Therefore, she made sure I spent most of my senior year in in-school suspension. Thanks to her, I finally graduated high school after one freshman year, one sophomore year, three attempts at junior year, and one senior year, not to mention all of the night classes and correspondence classes I'd had to take to catch up. It never even occurred to me to quit and just get my GED. I was going to graduate from high school; it was important to me to get my diploma.

I had wanted the experience of graduating high school so much, but my graduation ceremony itself was very bittersweet. My sister, who at first had been two grades below me, was a good student. She was graduating on time, which meant we graduated together. Her name comes before mine in the alphabet, so she got to cross the stage and graduate before me. That didn't sit well with me. It was supposed to be her day, not mine. We had a party afterward with the family and her friends, and I remember looking around at everyone in the house and wondering what I was doing there. I shouldn't have been there, taking her moment away from her. But if she was upset, she never said anything about it to me. Maybe, I thought, there was part of her that was happy for me. Maybe everyone in my family was breathing a sigh of relief. Probably not Triple B—for him, I knew, the fact that it had taken me this long was no doubt proof that I was what he had always thought me to be: a loser.

I had survived, and I had accomplished a small goal that had once seemed unreachable. I wasn't yet thinking about law school, or about the possibility of igniting that spark inside of me that yearned for stability, money, success. At twenty years old and after barely graduating high school with a 1.04 GPA and a class rank of 376 out of 380, college was not on my mind at all.

CHAPTER 3

New Friends, Same Old Story

In 1999, Congress was going through proceedings to impeach President Clinton, Google had just been founded, and I, a newly minted high school graduate, had decided it was time for me to lend the advanced skills I had acquired in my previous six years of high school to the real-world workforce.

I knew almost nothing about cars. Strike that. I knew *less than* nothing about cars. I barely had enough skill to drive them. (Some would say I didn't even do that very well.) I wasn't sure how they worked, and I sure as hell didn't know how to fix them. So of course I got a job at a ten-minute oil-change place, where I learned how to drain the oil and replace the filter. I had learned the craft at another quickie lube place during one of my high school expulsions. The pay was decent, and I was able to work forty hours a week or more if I wanted. My drug-dealing days, I hoped, were far behind me.

Customers would roll in through the garage doors guided by me or an inattentive mechanic wannabe. They'd ask me questions about their transmission or carburetor and I never had any idea what they were talking about. I'd just nod and offer a "Hmmmm" or "Interesting," so it seemed like I had a grasp of mechanic knowledge. My go-to line was, "It could be a number of things. You know how they put computers in cars these days." That usually stopped the conversation. If they inquired further, I got the supervisor, who was more than happy to pretend he knew what he was talking about. Thankfully, most of the customers who brought their cars in didn't know much about them either.

It didn't take long for me to get bored: Drain the oil, replace the filter, replace the old oil with new. Rinse and repeat. The oil-change place was a temporary gig, something to help me earn cash while I figured out my next step. What I really needed was something that challenged my mind, or at the very least something that was different. I wondered whether Mr. Brady and Mr. Bishop had been right. After finishing a long shift, reeking of motor oil and exhausted beyond belief, I started to wonder: Was I really capable of more? Did I even think I *deserved* more?

One day, as I was working under a Ford Taurus in the "the pit", watching the black used oil leak from the car and down the drain, I felt my life heading in the same direction. I needed to experience something different and didn't want to spend the rest of my life changing northeast Ohio's oil. After my tenure in high school, I wasn't really sure if I had what it took to go to college, but suddenly, I was willing to find out. But is going back to school even the answer to what I want to change? I asked myself. And could I even get into college?

Society told me I should go to college if I wanted to be successful and happy, and I wanted to be both of those things. I was, suddenly, sure that if I could just graduate from college, my life would be perfect. I could get a well-paying job, find a nice girl, buy a home, and start a family, all like a normal person. At least that's what I thought I wanted. Plus, I wanted to prove to myself and everyone I was capable of more, at least to those who thought my life wouldn't amount to much. Still, the fears that had held me back in high school were not far below the surface—the possibility of rejection, what people would think of me if that happened, almost prevented me from even trying. But I threw caution to the wind and decided college would be my next step.

The first step in the process was taking the ACT. By the time I had gotten tired of coming home smelling like motor oil every night, most high school graduates who were college bound had already done this and were actually attending college. In my sixth year of high school, I had been so busy focusing on actually getting that elusive diploma that I'd decided to forgo taking the ACT. But now I had to rectify that.

I didn't study at all; in fact, the night before the ACT, I decided the best thing to do was go out drinking with my buddies. I woke up the next morning to the sound of my alarm blaring on my nightstand. I slapped the button to shut it up. I had a pounding headache and almost just rolled over and went back to sleep. But something dragged me out of bed that morning. I picked up my dirty, cigarette-smelling clothes from the night before, threw them on, and stumbled to my car. Barely making it to the testing site on time, I took my seat, and a few hours later, it was all over.

I left and forgot all about it, thinking my higher education was a worthless cause. I went on with my life, changing oil and mostly forgetting about my desire to go to college.

Before I took the ACT, I had done some research and discovered that the University of Akron wasn't all that selective when accepting students—it sounded like my kind of school! I had applied and signed up to have my ACT scores sent there. So when I received a letter with the University of Akron emblem on it a few weeks later, all of my thoughts and desires about going to college came rushing back. I tore the letter open. "Dear Mr. Robinson, we are excited to inform you . . . ," it began.

I didn't read the rest of the letter; I didn't have to. I was overjoyed. My life was about to change forever. To me, it felt like I had gotten into Harvard. I had a chance, an opportunity to improve my life, and I wasn't going to let it slip away. I had to prove to everyone that I had what it took to go to college, especially Triple B. Hell, I had to prove it to myself. I quit the oil-change place shortly after that.

At the time I was still living at home, with Triple B, but the situation was no longer tenable. We maintained a fragile sort of peace: If he came into the living room while I was watching TV, I'd wait just long enough to leave so it didn't seem like I was leaving because of him. He would do the same. I didn't like watching TV with him anyway, since he'd just get angry and start yelling at the news. But even elsewhere in the house, we never stayed in the same room together. I was eager to get the hell away from Triple B as soon as possible, but I was also just ready to be on my own. I got that reason when I received my acceptance letter. I immediately moved into a place right off the Akron campus with some guys who were also trying to make a go at college. I rarely went back home after I moved out, even though it was only a ten-minute drive away. I didn't like being there, and I wanted to feel like I was far enough away that I was really on my own.

It was an exciting time for me because the guys I lived with all wanted to do well in college, and we fed into that and supported each other. I majored in political science because it seemed like an easy track without an abundance of math and science courses, and I was mildly interested in the field. We had a map of the school on the wall where we marked all our classes with thumbtacks and we studied together almost nightly. We were setting ourselves up for success, and

I was excited. I loved being in the college scene, loved the idea of being around so many people trying to become better and do better. Just being on a college campus gave me goosebumps, because there seemed to be so many possibilities.

Before classes even started, I had my sights set on a higher goal than just attending and graduating from the University of Akron. I considered Akron a stepping stone. I really wanted to attend Kent State University. It was a better school with a much better reputation than Akron. Also, it was farther away from my hometown and farther from all my old friends.

Given my pre-college academic background, I knew I would have to do really well in my first semester at Akron in order to transfer to Kent. I decided to quit smoking weed, cut down on the drinking, and study my ass off. In doing so, I learned that if I actually paid attention in class and did the work, my grades would reflect that.

Lo and behold, it worked! I did really well. I did better than really well, in fact. I got straight A's and made the dean's list during my first semester of college. I had never done that well in high school, middle school, or even elementary school. After taking six years to graduate from high school, I was excelling in college. *I fucking knew it*, I thought. That report card was validation that I was capable of so much more. I was so happy to tell Mom and pretty much anyone else who would listen. Mom even put my report card up on the fridge at her home. I never heard from Triple B—not one word of congratulation. Nobody seemed as impressed as me, though, and there wasn't Facebook at the time, so I couldn't announce to the whole world what I had done. Shortly after, I applied to Kent State, was accepted, and continued my political science studies.

Kent State is only twenty or so minutes from Akron, so I packed up my belongings and headed east. I got a job working as a carhop at a burger joint called Swensons, which was pretty much the premier job to have in college at the time. I'd run out to the cars, take their orders, and then bring out their food. On a good week, I could take home almost $1,000 in cash. It was hard work, and it taught me that if I put in the effort, I could also reap the rewards. Of course I just pissed most of my earnings away, but in order to work at Swensons, I had to be in college and maintain a certain GPA. Both were loosely enforced, but it was another thing that would help me stay on track, even when it seemed like every other facet of my life was falling apart.

Working at Swensons was something of a status symbol since everyone at Kent State wanted a job there. I met a lot of great people there, including some who I'd stay in contact with decades later. Swensons was where I met Jeff, my future roommate and the person who introduced me to my Kent State friends. He also introduced me to a fraternity, Sigma Phi Epsilon, or Sig Ep as it was known. I had never considered myself a fraternity kind of guy, but it was an easy way to meet people and get into the college scene. It was fun to go to formal dances and other activities with the sororities. I was even a houseboy for a few semesters, a position that involved making dinner for all the girls in a sorority house. It was a great way to get a free dinner and meet girls. Plus, our frat house had amazing parties that were exclusive to members and pledges. I was getting the full college experience, which was one of the reasons I'd transferred to Kent in the first place.

I never officially joined the frat because I didn't finish the rush process. I didn't want to pay the fees involved, the kids I was rushing with were a lot younger than me, and even the guys who were guiding me through were younger than I was. I just had a hard time respecting the process. Even more importantly, I found another group of people that I related to more.

There were a bunch of guys who had either quit the frat or gotten kicked out who all got a house together right next door to the frat house. The house was painted baby blue and it came to be known as the Blu House. There was a total of eight frat "rejects" in the house. These guys liked to drink and smoke, so I was soon back at it. Still, they were good guys, not like my friends in high school. They supported me, cared about me, and took an actual interest in my life. They just weren't good for me. They were at the drinking and drug-use level that I had been at in high school. I had already gone through that stage, and I was about to go through it again with them.

Girlfriends would come and go again in college, but I still couldn't hold down a relationship. I had a brief relationship with Stacy, who I met through my roommate's girlfriend. She was at the sorority where I would sometimes "houseboy," and we hit it off. She would sleep over, and the relationship felt good—but then eventually I stopped calling and she did, too. The relationship just fizzled out.

I met another girl, Beth, from Swensons. She was really into me, but the more I sensed she liked me, the more I pushed her away. I know now that I just wasn't ready for what she wanted from me. I enjoyed her company, but to have someone want to spend all that time with me, to even start to envision a future with me, messed with my head. After years of tolerating emotional abuse—from Triple B and then from friends and girlfriends too—I didn't think I deserved love. Then I thought there must be something wrong with her if she was that into me. Unfortunately my destructive behavior extended to how I ended relationships, too—with Beth, I essentially ghosted her until she got the hint and moved on. I never felt good about it, especially when I would see her or my other ex-girlfriends out at the downtown bars with someone else. I just had real commitment and attachment issues that I didn't know how to handle. I was worried about being betrayed or rejected, and yet at the same time I didn't know how to truly open myself up to a loving relationship. What resulted was a lot of awkward endings and hurt feelings—including my own.

As I grew up, I always feared the worst was going to happen to me—because at four years old, it did when Triple B entered my life and I was completely helpless to do anything about it. At night, I'd lay in bed and just imagine terrible, unrealistic scenarios playing out in my head. For example, I was certain our house was going to burn down, so I'd go check the oven in the middle of the night to make sure it was off. As an adult I'd be scared I was going to lose my friends, my girlfriends, I'd be in financial ruin or worse—just waiting for the other shoe to drop, all based on nothing.

If I wanted better for myself, I'd have to become better first. But it would take me a long time to realize that.

In the meantime, too much of my time was occupied by the lavish (at least by college standards) parties we threw at Blu House and the different houses we lived in over the years. The consequences of all that partying were rough—both on the houses and on my grades. We managed to trash the Blu House so badly that the landlord sued us all for damages. Admittedly, it was really bad: doors were broken down, the carpet was soaked with beer, and we never once cleaned the entire place. And unlike at Akron, where I'd made the dean's list, at Kent State I never came close. In fact, I was on academic probation for most of my time there. Once, they tried to kick me out for my poor grades, and I had to write a letter to the dean explaining why they should let me stay in school. Still, I kept at it, going to school all throughout the year, even during the summer. I knew deep down that if I took off even one semester, I wouldn't go back.

So one semester at a time, I somehow managed to limp through to my senior year of college. The finish line was within my sight—but little did I know that senior year, instead of propelling me into the post-grad life and career I'd dreamed of, would threaten to derail everything I'd been working toward.

The local college bars were only a few blocks from where we lived, but whenever we wanted to head down there, even if it was nice out, we usually drove. One early April afternoon in 2001, I decided to take my 1995 Jeep Wrangler down to the bar with three other people. We hit up Buffalo Wild Wings first and chugged some twenty-two-ounce Budweisers. Then it was on to Glory Days, where we drank many sugar-free Red Bull–and–vodkas—my drink of choice in college—as fast as we could. Finally, it was time to hit up Ray's Place, where we would spin their "shot wheel," which was similar to the one on Wheel of Fortune, except instead of numbers, it had different liquors. We all took multiple turns on the wheel, taking down shots of Fireball, Jägermeister, and Jack Daniel's. Back then, when I wasn't in class or working, I was drinking. And so we were getting hammered in the middle of the day for no real reason; we just felt like it.

After four or so hours of heavy drinking, it started to get dark out, and we wanted to go home and change our clothes so we could go back out and drink some more with a different crowd. I decided the smart thing to do was for me to drive us back to our house. *It's only a few blocks away. What could go wrong?* I thought. I'd made this drive dozens of times before in worse condition.

Four of us all piled into the Jeep, and I started blasting Oasis. Everything was going well; we were all laughing and singing "Wonderwall." Until we weren't.

I took a left turn onto University Drive, where we lived, from Main Street. I hit the gas hard, and before I knew it, chaos had ensued. There was a sudden impact and the crashing sound of my Jeep's front end imploding.

After the impact, I looked around and asked if everyone was okay. I didn't get much of a response. Two of my passengers simply jumped out and walked back to our place, which was only a half block away. I could see it from the scene of the accident. Then I looked over at the person in the passenger seat; she seemed to be fine. I wasn't physically hurt at all besides a few scratches.

I tried to restart my Jeep and get the hell out of there, but it wouldn't move. By this time, I could hear the sirens of the ambulance, police, and fire department on their way. The passenger who had stayed in the Jeep with me got out and went over to the ambulance when it pulled up. *I hope she's okay*, I thought.

I exited the Jeep and walked around to the front to assess what had happened. The front was completely smashed in around a telephone pole that was now leaning at a thirty-five-degree angle. As I had taken the turn, I had somehow accelerated the Jeep to almost forty miles per hour before crashing into the pole. As I stared at the carnage I had just created, I noticed that the blue-and-red lights from all the emergency vehicles were bouncing off the Jeep and the surrounding houses. They looked unusually bright, and it took me a moment to realize that was because when I took out the telephone pole, it had knocked out the electricity. I later learned that the outage had impacted a ten-block radius.

The next thing I noticed was two police officers headed straight toward me. "This your Jeep?" one of them asked as they approached.

"Yep," I quickly replied, feeling a bit dazed and knowing what was about to happen.

"And you were driving it?" the cop continued.

"Yep."

"How drunk are you?" the other officer finally asked. I guess they could tell by the smell on my breath and by how I was conducting myself. Not to mention the catastrophe behind me.

I turned around, looked at the Jeep, and then looked at the telephone pole. I faced the officers again and said, "Not drunk enough to cause this," pointing at my totaled Jeep. And I believed it.

"Turn around and put your hands on the hood," one of the officers commanded.

I complied, and they arrested me on the spot without even conducting a formal sobriety test. There was no need; I was clearly drunk. They placed me in the cop car with my hands cuffed behind my back. As I sat locked in the police cruiser, I saw the girl who hadn't walked back to my place head for the hospital in an ambulance. I was growing concerned for her well-being. *God, I hope she's okay,* I thought. *I hope everyone is okay.*

As I watched the scene unfold from the backseat of the cop car, with more police and firemen showing up by the minute and the red-and-blue lights bouncing off my totaled Jeep, I realized that my cell phone was still in my back pocket. They had searched me but didn't take my phone for some reason.

I managed to wriggle the flip phone out of my pocket and throw it on the seat beside me. I leaned over and dialed the first person who came to my mind: Mom. I almost had to lie down on the seat to put my ear to the phone because I couldn't use my cuffed hands.

"Mom, I need you to meet me at the Kent police station," I slurred over the phone.

"What's going on?" she asked. It sounded like I had woken her up.

"There's been an accident. Please meet me there." And with that, I hung up.

I was transported to the police station and put in a holding cell. I kept inquiring about all the passengers in my Jeep and was told that everyone was at the hospital getting treated, even the two who had left the scene on foot. Eventually, I was released on my own recognizance and saw my sister and mom in the police station lobby in tears. I hadn't even needed to call Mom to be released. But I was scared and didn't know what was going to happen.

I begged Mom to take me to the hospital so I could see my friends who had been in the Jeep with me. She tried to talk me out of it, but I insisted. As it turned out, she was probably right. I wasn't prepared for what was waiting for me there. Everyone's parents and family members were attending to their respective kids, and they were not happy to see me. They were all staring me down; they wouldn't even talk to me. I apologized to everyone as best I could and left shortly after.

That night, I felt shame, embarrassment, and regret. *Maybe Triple B was right about me all along*, I thought. Thankfully, nobody was permanently injured, though I'm sure some of them have lasting effects from that night. I know I do.

I was charged with driving under the influence (DUI) and reckless operation of a vehicle. It could have been a lot worse, especially if someone had been seriously injured. This time I decided not to represent myself and hired a lawyer who specialized in college kids charged with DUIs. We went to court, and the prosecutor offered to drop the reckless operation charge if I pled guilty to driving under the influence, which I did. I had to pay court costs, got a suspended license for a year, and had to spend a weekend at an intervention program.

The intervention program took place at a local Holiday Inn, where I met with counselors and attended AA meetings. For the second time in my life, I was in some sort of drug rehab, and this time, it had been forced upon me. In order to get released from the program, I needed to talk about how my drinking was a problem and promise to not drink again; only then would they allow me to go on with my life. I said what they wanted to hear, but the truth was, not much changed after my DUI. It should have been a big wake-up call, and in some respects it was. But only for a moment. I suppressed the memories and feelings the accident stirred up and pretended none of it was a big deal. A lot of kids get DUIs in college, I told myself; I normalized what wasn't normal.

It wasn't that I hated college; I actually liked being in class. I had one political science professor whose class I especially liked because it didn't feel like I was going to listen to another boring lecture. Instead, her discussions made me feel like I was going there to hear a really great story, or to get a fascinating perspective on the world, no matter the topic. She was very kind to me and reminded me of my grandmother. She would stay after class and patiently answer all my questions. She even offered to write me a letter of recommendation if I ever decided to apply to graduate school. *Fat chance*, I thought, but I appreciated the gesture.

Another political science professor was understanding when, after my DUI, I needed an extension for a project that was due. While I was in his office, he had a talk with me about running with a different crowd in college. Again, I appreciated the attention. But his wisdom didn't stick.

Pretty soon I was back in the swing of things, partying every night. Instead of calming down with the drinking and drug use, I decided to ratchet it up. Tuesdays became our cocaine night, dubbed "tutting Tuesdays," where we would do coke all night until we ran out. I pulled all-nighters constantly, but it was never to study or get a paper done; it was to do coke. I made excuses for my drug use: everyone was doing it; I was in college now, so it was okay; at least I was trying to make something of myself. I also rationalized it because I wasn't selling drugs this time. Somehow, that made me a better person. It was almost like high school all over again, except I wasn't getting into as many fights, and I was now legally allowed to drink.

It was easy for me to get sucked into unhealthy patterns, mostly because I didn't have any healthy patterns. I made bad decisions, suffered consequences—and then just kept making more bad decisions. It was a cycle I'd gotten trapped in a long time ago, back in my middle school and high school days, when I'd been desperate for an escape from Triple B, and desperate also for any sort of social validation. But it wasn't a sustainable way to live—not then and not now. Before long, all these choices started to snowball on me. The bad decisions may not have been the easier route, but they seemed like an easier route for me. Plus, it was the route all my friends were taking.

Soon, I wanted to have the same feeling I'd had when I was selling drugs: having copious amounts of money and everyone wanting to get ahold of me and be around me. In reality, I just wanted to be wanted and feel significant. My solution was to start gambling. And not just regular gambling; no, I would be a bookie and take other people's bets. I focused on college and pro football, though during baseball playoffs I also took some bets. If there was a chance I'd make money, I'd take the bet. Prior to this, I was familiar with how sports odds and spreads worked. I occasionally gambled on games and liked to watch sports. However, when I was making bets on my own, I usually lost and had to pay the bookie a lot of money. At one point, I thought to myself, *I should be the one taking bets*.

Being a bookie wasn't everything I thought it would be, though. I don't think I was very good at it because I wasn't really making any money. I was even cheating the system at times by adjusting the spreads and the odds, but that just made matters worse. I'd either owe a lot of money or I'd have friends upset with me because they now owed me a lot of money. Also, I had no real way to force people to pay me back. Sometimes I'd get mad at friends if we were out and they were buying drinks even though they owed me money on a bet. It was an easy way to lose friends and make people not like me.

My only saving grace was that I was making decent money at Swensons. But it was a shitty feeling having to pick up extra shifts just to pay back gambling debts.

Finally, after four years of college, I graduated with a political science degree and an impressive 2.02 GPA. The only reason I was able to graduate college at all was because despite all of the drinking, partying, bookmaking, and coke-fueled all-nighters, I attended classes every single day, save the day I got my DUI.

The day of the graduation ceremony, I drove to the arena where it would be held, parked my car, and pulled out a joint to celebrate. I got high by myself in my car before walking across the stage, so

I don't remember most of it. I don't even know who the keynote speaker was, or what they talked about.

That evening, Mom had a huge party at my house against Triple B's wishes. We rented a tent and got a keg. I invited everyone I knew to show them what I had accomplished; I was proud. I invited my old high school principals and teachers, but none of them showed. I had managed to graduate from college before all of my high school friends. I thought it was quite an accomplishment — Triple B didn't think so, he didn't say a word to me at the party and mostly kept to himself that night, which was the best case scenario for me.

With a college degree in hand, I was now ready to go out into the "real" workforce. However, I had a few problems: no job prospects, a dismal GPA, and no connections. Once the high of graduation wore off, I was forced to take a job working construction with one of my friends, Carl, at his father's company.

This was a really low point in my life. We would get up every morning, get coffee, stop by the job site, do nothing, leave at ten a.m. to go to McDonald's or whatever fast-food joint was open and chow down, sleep in the truck, do an hour of work, and then go straight to the bar. This routine went on for the better part of a year, and I gained about fifty pounds. At one point, I was pushing the scale at over two hundred pounds (I'm about five foot ten inches tall on a good day). I didn't feel good about myself or about my life. During this time, I was applying for "real" jobs but didn't have any "real" work experience, so nothing came along.

What I needed, I thought, was to take a big leap. For a while I'd had dreams of living in New York City—I'd even told people at my graduation party that I would be moving out there, even though I had no job lined up and no idea where I'd live. I wasn't faring much better in Ohio, though, so I decided to give the Big Apple a shot. Pretty much as soon as my bus stopped in Penn Station, I knew I was in over my head. I had under $1,000 to my name, and the only apartments I could afford were in Spanish Harlem or East Harlem. I eventually found a place and paid $600 cash for the first month's rent. When I arrived, though, I found that it was just a room—I was sharing a kitchen, living room, and bathroom with a dozen other people, all of whom spoke only Spanish. As soon as I got there, I went into my bedroom and cried. I felt like I had already failed. Not long afterward, I moved back to Ohio with my tail between my legs.

I crashed with a friend in Kent for a while as I applied for more jobs. I found a temporary gig with a political action committee out of D.C. that had me traveling to different college campuses registering students to vote. I went to UMass, Cornell, Amherst, Temple, the University of Vermont. I liked traveling, talking to the students, and getting to know lots of new people staying with host families in each city. But once the election ended in November, so did the job.

Then one day, my high school friend Brad, who was living in San Francisco at the time, gave me a call. His roommate was moving out, he now had an extra room, and he wanted to know if I wanted to move in. He didn't have to ask twice. I immediately agreed to go live in California. After all, what else was I going to do? I had accomplished my immediate goal, to graduate college, and yet I was still unsatisfied. I was already thinking of where I might wander, what I could do to ignite that spark that existed inside of me, and California seemed like the ultimate escape. Not owning much of anything, I packed up a suitcase and started the lonely cross-country drive.

CHAPTER 4
Wherever I Go, There I Am

It was 2004, and I was on my way to San Francisco in a run-down 1995 black four-door Volkswagen Jetta that I'd purchased with the insurance money I got from totaling my Jeep in college. The Jetta, like me, was a bit of a mess. The transmission was about to go, the engine constantly overheated, and there were several electrical problems, including the windshield wipers not working. I couldn't fix any of these mechanical issues, but if the car needed an oil change or washer fluid, I was on top of it.

I was concerned that it might not make it all the way to California, but I didn't really have any other options. I needed to get out there quickly because rent was due, and I was already a few days late. California felt like a new start for me, and I was rushing toward it as fast as my rickety Jetta could take me there, hoping—and needing—to leave my past behind.

Driving that distance alone for the first time wasn't as enjoyable as I thought it would be. In my head, I had imagined the windows down, the radio turned up, and the miles churning by as I let my bright and lucrative future call me forward. In reality, though, it was a complete nightmare. Because I was in such a rush to get out there, I had to sacrifice sleep for driving. A little over halfway through my trip, I pulled over and took a brief forty-five-minute "nap" at a rest stop somewhere in Nebraska on Interstate 80. The break was more to give my eyes a chance to rest from all the windshield time than anything else. Unfortunately, I wasn't able to fall asleep because I was so uncomfortable from not being able to lie down. Plus, I was parked in a noisy rest area in the middle of the day. *If only I had a van I could sleep in*, I thought.

After my failed attempt at a nap, I decided to get back on the road, chugging as much Red Bull and coffee as I could along the way.

There were times when the radio couldn't pick up a signal and just played static, and I had nobody to talk to. The silence bothered me, so I resorted to talking to myself. To pass the time, I played solitaire on the laptop that was open on my passenger seat. I had my right hand on my laptop, while I steered with my left. My left hand also held a Camel menthol light cigarette, which I was chain-smoking. Somewhere in Utah, I picked up my cell phone and noticed it was dead. I didn't have a car charger. I was navigating via printed directions from MapQuest, and I got lost several times in Nevada. This was before everyone had GPS. I was going out of my mind from boredom, and I would have rather had my worst enemy sitting next to me to share the empty silence.

To add insult to injury, it started raining in Wyoming. I thought I might still be able to drive without the wipers because I had applied a rain repellent to the windshield, but the police thought otherwise. As I was driving along in the pouring rain, I looked out my rearview mirror and saw the blue and red flashing lights I'd become so familiar with over the years. I immediately panicked and tried to remember if I had any drugs in the car. It was an automatic reaction. Luckily, I didn't have anything illegal. Then for a brief moment, I had to ask myself if I was sober. Yes, I was sober—but exhausted.

The cop directed me to pull over to the side of the road until the rain stopped, thus prolonging my trip even more. I explained to him that I needed to get out to California in a hurry to pay my rent. He didn't care. "Would you rather arrive dead or late?" he said as he handed me a ticket. He mumbled something about my safety and the safety of others on the road. The rain finally subsided twenty minutes later, and I was on my way again.

After fifty or so hours on the road, I was welcomed to San Francisco via the Bay Bridge. I drove through the small tunnel that led to the bridge and held my breath until I saw San Francisco's skyline slowly come into view. To my right was the pyramid top of the Transamerica building; below me was the "Port of San Francisco" sign welcoming me; and ahead of me, off in the distance, was the Sutro Tower, settled on a hill between Twin Peaks and Mount Sutro, as well as my new future. Immediately, my adrenaline started pumping. I was overwhelmed and relieved that I was finally here. Crossing that bridge was like crossing over into a new life. I had finally arrived, tired, overweight, and a bit delirious, but I'd made it after all. The drive might have been miserable, but I had never second-guessed my choice to go out to California. Before California, all I had done was wander across my home state of Ohio not far from home, had a temporary job that took me to a few colleges in different states, and made a brief, failed attempt at making it in New York City. There was nothing for me in Ohio but bad news and regret, and I was far more excited about the possibilities that awaited me here.

I made my way into the city and drove toward my new home, navigating the steep hills with palm trees lining the roads. Driving under the speed limit, I tried to soak in the sun and my new surroundings. In addition to Brad, I'd be living with another roommate, Mary, who was just a friend of Brad's. The apartment was in a good area, Noe Valley, in the heart of San Francisco—it had a nice balcony where we had a great view of the city. The nickname for their neighborhood was "Stroller Valley" on account of all the yuppies and their kids living there.

As soon as I arrived at my new place, I was forced to wait even longer to start my new life as I drove around the block several times looking for a parking spot. Finally, I spotted a car leaving and made my move. I parked and dragged myself up toward the four-unit apartment with dark brown wooden shingles and a red roof. I pressed the doorbell, and Brad came down to open up the gate. I didn't say much, I just handed him my rent check and asked where my room was. Taking my suitcase, he led me to my new empty room with a view of the house next to us. I could literally open the window and touch the exposed red bricks of our neighbor's place. Not having much to unpack, I went to sleep on the floor of my new room for fifteen hours straight. All I owned was my car, a suitcase of clothes, my computer, and my cell phone. When I woke up, it was time to start my life in a new city where nobody knew me. The only problem was that I'd brought myself with me. The first thing I did as a new citizen of San Francisco was head to Zeitgeist, a bar in the Mission District with an outdoor patio littered with picnic tables. We ordered pitchers of beer and drank the day away to celebrate my arrival.

The next morning, I woke up on the floor of my empty room hungover. In the cold light of day, the reality of my romantic trip out west became clear: I was broke and needed to get a job ASAP. Not only did I have to start paying rent monthly, my college loans were coming due and it looked like I was going to keep up my old lifestyle of partying. It seemed that I had put myself back into a corner. If I didn't find a job, I wasn't going to be able to live out here too long. The next step would be living on the streets or living in my Jetta. I couldn't go back home, and I had nowhere else to go. At least if I was going to be homeless, San Francisco was the place to do it. With a fairly mild temperature and the ocean nearby, it could have been worse.

In truth, the rampant homelessness in San Francisco was quite a shock to me when I first arrived compared to Ohio. On every block, there seemed to be at least one homeless person with a sign asking for help. It was more prevalent in Haight-Ashbury and downtown, but Noe Valley still had its share. As with anything else, I got used to it and gave them money whenever I could.

At the time, the hotel unions were striking, and I was happy to take advantage of the situation and cross the picket line to become a scab. I went downtown to the best hotel in San Francisco—the Four Seasons—applied, and was hired the next day as a bellhop. This wasn't exactly what I'd gone to college for, but I was grateful to have an income. Plus, I knew the job would last only as long as the strike did.

Every day, I had to cross the picket line to go to work. The dozens of striking union members shouted, "Scab! Scab!" at me as I walked into the hotel. It wasn't the most positive or uplifting way to start my day, but I didn't let it get to me too much—I had a paycheck, which I badly needed. Besides, pretty much everything was a new experience to me so I took it all in stride.

Being a bellhop was easy and interesting. The hotel served breakfast to all employees every morning for free, and during the day, all I had to do was bring people's bags up to their room—that's it. They'd tip me for it, too. Not only was I getting a paycheck, I was also getting a free breakfast and leaving with cash tips in hand. I had to wear the stereotypical bellhop uniform with the black hat that looked like something a chauffeur would wear, along with a dark gray coat with dozens of gold buttons sewed to the front, but it was a small price to pay for having an income.

I didn't understand at the time why the union workers would even want to strike; it seemed to me that they had it pretty good, what with the free breakfast and tips, and I was happy for their strike to provide me with an opportunity. I see now I was only doing the job for several weeks, and I wasn't depending on the income to support a family. If I'd had to keep doing it for a living, I could certainly have understood their asking for better wages.

While I was working as a bellhop, I was also trying to find a more permanent job somewhere before the strike ended. I knew I could be a server and that I could find that type of job fairly easily. Eventually, I got a waiter job at Tony Roma's rib joint in Embarcadero Center downtown.

Embarcadero was a multilevel shopping center spanning four blocks right by the water, which attracted a lot of tourists. The waiter job soon turned into a bartending gig, which meant I was making even more money. I apparently moved up so quickly because I had impressed management by actually showing up on time and not calling in sick. I guess being on time was a rarity in California. In fact, everybody there was on "California time," which meant showing up ten or fifteen minutes late. Having grown up in the Midwest, I subscribed to the philosophy of "To be early is to be on time, to be on time is to be late, and to be late is unacceptable."

I was actually making really good money bartending. At the time, the minimum wage in San Francisco was close to $9 an hour, and in addition to the hourly rate, I was making tips. This meant that I was able to pay my rent, start paying back my student loans, and even save a little money. This was the first time I had ever been able to get my financial situation at least somewhat in order. Before that, my credit score had been in the tank because I'd defaulted on my student loans and cosigned for some of my friends' cell phones in high school, which they'd never paid for.

I could have continued being a bartender and living in San Francisco forever. I had money in my pocket and little stress. I really enjoyed the San Francisco lifestyle. I ended up selling my Jetta because parking was a nightmare, and I didn't need it because the mass transit was amazingly reliable.

The days started melting into one another, and I could feel myself getting into a groove. Brad and I spent a lot of time with our neighbors, or I would have co-workers over at our place to drink and get high after work. We would all play poker and then go over to The Valley Tavern, a local bar where our roommate Mary worked.

Our apartment was walking distance to Dolores Park, and on my days off I would walk over there to people watch and be alone with my thoughts. I was having fun in San Francisco, but I couldn't shake the nagging fear in the back of my mind that I would wake up one day, forty years old, and still be a bartender. Not that there was anything wrong with that. But I didn't want to spend the next two decades drinking, smoking, and playing cards—the same way I'd spent most of my high school years. That wasn't something I wanted for my life, and I tried to snap myself out of the routine I was getting so used to. It was the small feeling I'd gotten when I decided to leave the oil-change place and apply to college. *There has to be something more for me.* While my living situation was great for the time being, it didn't really lend itself to personal growth. Although I was relatively happy, I wasn't living up to my full potential, which is what I aspired to do.

The only thing that was growing in my apartment was pot. My roommates liked to grow weed, so I got back into smoking weed again. I was pretty much in a constant daze, and I knew I'd had enough. I knew myself, and I knew I needed a change. In my mind, I still hadn't proved to myself and to all my haters that I was good enough. I still didn't feel like a success. Of course, it was hard to feel like a success when I was bartending during the day and getting high and drunk at night several times a week. All of those cycles I'd let myself fall into during my high school and college years were repeating. I dated a few girls during my time in San Francisco, including someone from work who I really liked. Still, I wasn't ready for a serious relationship. We got into a big fight when she wanted to keep our relationship a secret from our co-workers and I didn't want to. Then, when things got too serious, I broke her heart. Apparently it didn't matter what city I was in; when it came to romance, I was still a bit of a jerk.

One day I was bartending at Tony Roma's when a regular named Ralph came in for lunch. He was an older, heavyset man with slicked back gray hair who worked in the skyscrapers right outside the restaurant in the Embarcadero. I didn't know him well, but from what I understood, he was some type of big money, high-powered lawyer.

Usually he requested Dana as his server, but Dana was off on this particular day and so it was my responsibility to serve him. He ordered shrimp prawns—his regular order, I later found out—but I put in for shrimp scampi. When I brought out the wrong dish, he lost his mind. I had never seen a customer so upset. I don't remember everything he said while he was ranting and raving, but one line stuck out.

"You need to know your *craft*," he shouted. "If you don't know the difference between shrimp prawns and shrimp scampi, you're not going to make it very far here."

I was blown away. *My craft?! We're not saving lives here,* I thought. This was a bartending gig, not something that I wanted to turn into a career. I didn't give a fuck about the shrimp, but his perception of me bothered me to no end. Did he really think this was the limit of my ambition? Did others think that, too?

All of a sudden I felt exhausted. I didn't want to listen to another customer who thought they were better than me or talked down to me. I played my part with Ralph, taking his abuse and apologizing profusely for my mistake, but what I wanted to say to him was, *I could be a lawyer too, you know!* Or I wanted to tell him I had a college degree. But that didn't matter—there were people with college degrees who had been working at the restaurant for years. Nothing would change how customers like Ralph saw me and my colleagues. What I needed, I realized in that moment, was to leave. I couldn't do this job for the rest of my life.

What could I do to make myself happy and feel like a success and make others think I'm a success too? I thought over the days and weeks that followed. As much as I was driven by my own internal discontent, when it came to fixing the problem, my focus was still on what other people thought about me, which was misplaced. But I didn't know any better at the time. I thought the answer was to make a lot of money. *What profession could I pursue that makes a lot of money?* I thought of Ralph, and then I also thought of that courtroom so long ago, a nervous fuck-up teenager finding his voice. The answer came easily: law. But was it even possible for me to get into law school? I had barely passed my classes in high school and college, and had multiple arrests on my record. *Do they let criminals become lawyers?* It seemed like an enormous risk, a leap of faith, really. But just as I'd determined San Francisco was the way to go, I convinced myself that law school would be the answer to all my problems. I'd finally get the approval of Triple B, be happy, have money, and achieve society's version of success.

Before I got ahead of myself with all of my dreaming of the future, I needed to make some practical changes here in the present.

Financially, I was pretty well set to pick up and move wherever this next part of my journey would take me. That was one of the ways in which San Francisco had been good for me.

The first big step I knew I had to take, though, was to quit smoking weed—so I quit that cold turkey along with cigarettes. There was no way I could be a stoner and a law student.

Next I needed to take the LSAT, the law school entrance exam. The LSAT contained five parts, one of which was given twice: logical reasoning, analytical reasoning, reading comprehension, and an essay question. A perfect score on the LSAT was a 180, and back when I was applying to law school, a score of 155 would grant you acceptance to some schools. I went back to my ACT days and took the test without studying. I didn't even get close to a 150. I took the test again, studying a bit on my own beforehand, and again didn't do well. Finally, I knew I had to do something different; after all, getting accepted into law school is a different game. I enrolled in an LSAT prep class and took the test a third time.

This time, I did well enough to get accepted to Thomas M. Cooley Law School at Western Michigan, located in Lansing, Michigan. Cooley gets a bad rap because it's not a top-tier law school. But my options were limited. It was an accredited law school willing to give me a chance, and I was grateful for the opportunity.

As part of the application process, I had to inform the school of all my criminal conduct, from juvenile to adult, even if I was never arrested, convicted, or even caught. I was to notify the school of all these incidents because, after graduation, when I applied to the bar, I'd have to pass a "character and fitness" evaluation to see whether I was fit to be a lawyer. At that point, I would be asked to provide the state bar with the same information. With my questionable past and dismal college GPA, I thought my application would simply be thrown in the garbage, but, by some stroke of luck, I was accepted. However, the fact that the character and fitness evaluation was part of the bar exam haunted me every day of law school and I was living in fear. I was afraid that I was wasting my time because even if I made it through law school, I wouldn't be able to pass the character and fitness exam to become a licensed attorney. The fear ate me up inside on a daily basis.

After only two short years in San Francisco, I moved back to the Midwest in the summer of 2006. My new destination was Lansing, Michigan, only a three-hour drive from my hometown of Cuyahoga Falls. This time, though, I flew cross-country, leaving behind most of the belongings I had acquired in California.

Succeeding in law school was very different from succeeding in college, and I would need to do much more than just attend classes if I wanted to stay and pass. When I was an undergrad, I'd known how to play the game in order to get my degree. Law school was a different game entirely, and I didn't know the rules. I wasn't prepared. I hadn't been in school in over three years, and I didn't even know how to really study. Most of my classmates were younger, coming right out of college, and computer savvy. I hadn't done anything on a computer in quite some time other than play online poker and mess around on Myspace. Now I had to learn to use a computer as a study aid.

Luckily I learned quickly, and I already knew how to type. I was serious about taking a different approach in law school. Because I didn't know how to succeed, I thought I would hang around the students who did know how to excel in school. To that end, I found the smartest kids in our class, Brent and Dalton, and stuck to them like decal advertisements on a NASCAR stock car.

Brent and Dalton were amazing study partners and amazing friends. They helped me stay focused, do the work, and put in long hours at the library. Most importantly, they didn't party a lot, so when I was with them, I was focused and clear headed. They showed me how to create outlines for my classes, and we spent so much time teaching each other the law on a huge dry-erase board in empty classrooms on campus that we eventually had the subjects memorized and knew it like the backs of our hands.

It wasn't just my memory skills that were enhanced, either. Law school taught me a different way of thinking, where not everything is black and white. It taught me to question everything, and to see situations and issues from all sides. Everything needed to be analyzed using the IRAC method:

Issue—What is the issue here?

Rule—What is the law that is applicable to the situation?

Analysis—How is the law applied to the issue at hand?

Conclusion—Why should a certain situation or set of facts be ruled on in a certain way?

My first semester in law school went okay, with me earning a B− average. And I thought, *That's not too bad for a kid who shouldn't even be in law school. At least I'm not failing out.* And that wasn't nothing—kids were failing out of law school left and right. I'd always known in my heart that I was smart enough; now that I was around the "smart kids," I felt comfortable and was soaking everything in.

I was pleased with my B− average, so I decided to take on a heavier course load next semester with the thought of getting out of law school earlier.

The problem was, when I wasn't with Brent and Dalton, I was hanging around people who drank a lot. We had season tickets to Michigan State football and tailgated every game. My grades suffered. In fact, I failed a class during my second semester and barely passed the others. When I got my grades back that semester, I sat at my desk in my room, almost in tears. *What am I going to do?* I had put a lot of pressure on myself to succeed in law school. Also, what would everyone else think? *No big surprise there. Kyle failed out of law school.* I felt like I'd let myself down and that Triple B was right: I was a loser and a failure.

It wasn't just law school that was stressing me out. Shortly after I'd started at Cooley, I began dating a girl who lived near my hometown I met through my brother. She was younger than me, and beautiful—the main thing we had in common, I think, was that she didn't know much about how to have a real relationship, either. Sometimes she would drive up to see me, and I would enjoy showing her off to my roommates. When I would drive to see her outside of Cuyahoga Falls, I would also bring her to meet up with my high school friends. I didn't realize at the time they didn't care about me and would pretty much try to ruin my relationship if they thought they might have a shot with her.

Things got serious enough across that first year that I was sure we were in love. Unfortunately, I still didn't know how to have a real relationship. This one was filled with drama and constant fighting. Eventually we broke up, but we were still talking, and I wasn't ready to let her go.

Then one day I received a call from one of my best high school friends, Carl, who I worked with right after college at his dad's construction company.

"What's up?" I said, excited to chat.

"Listen, there's something I need to tell you," he said.

I knew this was serious because Carl never talked like this with me. I stood up from my kitchen table, leaving my bowl of oatmeal, and walked into my room. "What's going on?"

He proceeded to tell me that he was sleeping with my ex-girlfriend. I knew that he was well aware of how much I still cared about her since he was the one I had confided in about my breakup with her and how much it was affecting me. Instead of being a true friend, he'd gone and taken advantage of the situation.

The news hurt. I had been betrayed before by other friends, but I hadn't thought that Carl was capable of doing it, too. I already had a hard time trusting friends, and girlfriends, and this felt like a stake to the heart. I spent the next several months trying to get my ex back, just to stick it to Carl, which I eventually did. But it didn't make me feel any better. It was my ego that took a hit and that I was trying to salvage. I cared for her but we weren't really in love.

I was starting to realize that I needed to work on myself more than I needed to work on any of my existing relationships. I needed to be able to pursue romantic relationships not based on superficial things like looks or sex or how a partner would make others perceive me. For me, getting things right takes extra time—I learned that in high school, and with all of the wandering that had led me to law school.

It took me even longer to come to grips with the fact that I'd been a victim of abuse, and to get a handle on how that affected my life and my relationships. It would take even longer for me to realize I could have the life I wanted—I just needed to go inside and work on myself, stop running away and looking for distractions. And find friends who, unlike Carl, truly cared about me and wanted the best for me.

Although this situation was stressful, there was a silver lining: I focused on school more to keep my inner thoughts from taking over, stuck with Brent and Dalton, and turned my grades around after that terrible second semester. I started to find my groove inside the law school classroom.

I especially liked the classes that seemed to have a clear application to the real world. "Business Organizations" and "Tax" might not sound like the most thrilling courses, but I enjoyed them. Of course I had no idea that one day I'd be pulling out the outlines I created for those classes in order to start my own business. The tax professor was a younger guy with glasses and black hair—I think I liked his class, too, because he was closer to me in age than any of the other professors. He had a way of teaching that was applicable in the real world where other law school courses could get dragged down in the murky world of theory. The examples he used made it easy for me to envision applying the concepts we learned in the real world.

That class was a nice break from other courses, like "Evidence" and "Civil Procedure," which came off to me the same way calculus had in high school. It seemed entirely inaccessible, and I couldn't picture myself in any of the few situations that our professors used as examples. Then there was the professor for my torts class. He was older and always had a red face—from drinking, went the rumor. Another rumor had it that he was related to one of the board members, and that's how he'd gotten the job many years ago. In any case, it was clear to all us students that he hadn't represented a client in decades. I knew this wasn't Harvard Law and every professor couldn't be like my tax or my business organizations professor.

By my last semester of law school, I made the dean's list and even earned a certificate of merit for getting the highest grade in a class – Pre-Trial Skills. That class involved writing a brief, doing research, and then presenting your case in a mock trial with a real judge—I wondered whether I did so well because, unlike many of my colleagues, I had already presented in front of a judge in real life.

I was so pleased with myself, and Mom was proud of me as well. I was sure that even Triple B would now recognize that I wasn't an idiot and that I was worthy of his love and acceptance. But that was not to be; I heard only crickets from him. I was slowly coming to the realization that I could discover the cure for cancer, and I would still never receive his acceptance or admiration.

Getting closer to graduation, I spent every day worrying about applying for and taking the bar exam because of what I would have to disclose about my past to the character and fitness board. To be able to sleep at night, I told myself that I wasn't even going to take the bar and assumed I would just find some job and have a Juris Doctor. It was an issue that few of my classmates would have been able to relate to. In fact, some of them already had an "in" at a family firm and knew they were set after law school. They walked around with a palpable confidence; as long as they got their piece of paper and passed the bar, they were set.

But me? I was clueless as to what would come next. My focus, from my first semester to my last, was just on passing, nothing more. I couldn't afford to let myself get distracted by looking too far ahead.

When I was a kid, dreaming about steady, safe, white-collar jobs that might lift me out of Ohio and far, far away from Triple B, I used to wonder how exactly people became doctors, lawyers, engineers. I figured there was an incredibly intense, arduous process that weeded out all but the most deserving, a select few. While it was true that a few people seemed to have their path paved in gold, what I really learned in law school was that all you needed to do was follow a certain process, jump through hoops, and you could accomplish whatever you wanted. My peers weren't necessarily smarter than me—some were and some weren't. But most of us were jumping through the same hoops together.

To actually graduate from law school, I was required to go through the final hoop of taking an externship at a law firm to learn real-life lawyering skills and be in a law firm environment. An externship is similar to an internship, except I didn't get paid. It was a classroom experience outside of the school, and I was able to earn school credit for working. I knew I didn't want to stay in Michigan and I definitely didn't want to go back to Ohio. Therefore, I only applied to externships in New York City. I still had a yearning to live there and I wanted to rectify my failed previous attempt at moving there. I heard back from a boutique matrimonial law firm, and they accepted me. Of course they did; they really wanted the free labor.

My brother agreed to give me a ride, and just like that, I was off to New York City. This time, I was going to New York City for the right reasons and I was determined not to fail. It seemed like there were endless possibilities there, where I could start a new life for myself. It was like San Francisco all over again, and I was still searching for something more in myself.

CHAPTER 5

Company Man

When I arrived in New York City in 2006, Sully had just landed the plane in the Hudson River, President Obama was about to be inaugurated as the first African American president, and I would soon start learning the harsh reality of law-firm life.

Right before I moved to New York City, I had found a place on Craigslist in Soho at 42 Howard Street, just a block from Chinatown in Manhattan. The ad claimed it was a furnished one-bedroom, in a three-bedroom apartment, for $900 a month, which sounded like an amazing deal for NYC at the time. I should have known then that something was fishy considering my last experience trying to move to the City. I sent the money, sight unseen, and again moved with only a suitcase of clothes. When I arrived, I quickly discovered why the rent was so affordable.

My brother dropped me off in front of my new apartment with suitcase in hand around nine that morning. I hugged him goodbye and watched him drive off into the distance as his SUV was swallowed up by a sea of yellow cabs. I turned towards the apartment and my new life. I took a deep breath, opened the front door and walked up the three flights of stairs to the unit and knocked on the door. After almost ten minutes of knocking, a short, pudgy, asian guy with dark hair named Ping finally answered. Noticing his disheveled hair and his constant yawning, it was clear that I had woken him. I shook his hand as he welcomed me inside the apartment and showed me around. The layout of the loft was essentially an open area with two bedrooms, one on each side, and a small kitchen right inside the door off the bathroom. I kept looking around for a third door that led to my bedroom, but it wasn't there. I thought this was odd, because there were only two bedrooms, and I knew there would be three people living there, including myself. Then I was directed toward my living space. Ping pointed to a loft bed in the living room separated by a partition and told me there's a slight issue. *Here we go again.* I thought. Upon further investigation, I saw there was someone sleeping in my bed! Ping explained it was a French foreign-exchange student and he was just staying here until I arrived. I was annoyed, but too exhausted to complain. Ping and I left to go grab breakfast while my former bed occupant packed up and left. I eventually got my bed but was still underwhelmed. However, I was there, and there was no turning back now.

I wouldn't be getting paid at the law firm because I was receiving course credit, and student loans could only pay for so much—this was New York City, after all—so I needed to find a job. As I had in San Francisco, I applied to be a server at several restaurants. I was rather taken aback when some places actually asked for a headshot just to get an interview—as if that had anything to do with your qualifications. Within a few days though, I got a job as a server at Applebee's. It was located downtown in Battery Park, just a stone's throw away from the World Trade Center. At the time, construction on the new building and memorial was still underway. Every day, the construction workers filed into Applebee's around noon with their hard hats and ordered lunch. Sometimes, they'd sneak in a beer or two.

My legal externship at the matrimonial law firm was on Fifth

Avenue in midtown Manhattan. It had two partners and one associate. I worked at the law firm during the week and at Applebee's on the weekend. During that period, I worked over a hundred days straight without a day off. At first I was hoping the firm would offer me a job after the externship. I quickly realized that they never had any intention of doing so.

My experience at the law firm was, to put it bluntly, awful. My work area was the size of a small closet, and it was just outside the office of Leon, one of the firm's partners. I am still haunted by the sound of Leon's voice calling me into his office on a daily basis just so he could hear himself talk. Leon was an older, heavyset, bald gentleman who wore sweaters every day over his button up collared shirt and when he walked looked like an injured penguin waddling around. He should have been retired already; he had made a fortune and wasn't doing much legal work in the firm at all. When I arrived, he seemed to claim me as his free labor assistant immediately.

As I arrived at the firm and walked to my work space outside his office, I would hear Leon's shrieking voice before I even set my bag down in the morning: "Kyle! You here yet? Get in here! Why are you so late?" He would shout this at me even though I got in before eight a.m. every day and didn't even have to be there until nine.

I quickly learned that I always needed to bring a notepad and pen into Leon's office so I could pretend to write down whatever nonsense he was spewing. It was never actually important and didn't have anything to do with the law, but he liked to see me take notes on what he said. Sometimes it was about a movie he had seen or a restaurant he had eaten at. I didn't learn anything about the law from him.

When I wasn't in Leon's office, the other partner, Barry, would give me contracts to proofread or send me on errands. The firm basically used me for my free access to Westlaw—a computer-based legal research website. Westlaw can be very expensive, but as a law student, I had access to it for free.

The lawyers were also billing their clients for the work I did. According to their invoices, I was worth $250 an hour. The attorneys were chasing down their clients to get paid more than they were actually trying cases. Billable hours was the name of the game.

On a typical day, I would go into the office and talk with Erin, the other part-time intern, and we would complain about the "work" we had to do. I was in charge of the Rosenberg file, which basically meant that I looked through all of the paperwork in accordion-style files for the answers to whatever Leon asked me about the clients. If he needed to know how much the Rosenbergs paid for rent in 1987, I would spend my day rifling through the files. Hours or days later, when I'd finally found what I needed, he would be surprised. "Oh, you're still working on that? No, no, no, I actually need you to find what bank they used for their mortgage in 1997, and what was their interest rate." And then I would be off to the files once more.

I would search the files all morning and then pick it up again after a salad and brie sandwich from Hale and Hearty. Nothing about my externship involved any real legal work; it was all administrative. If I had no assignment, I would just stare at my computer waiting for the day to end. One day, when Leon was out, Barry sent me downtown to file a motion with the court. It was the New York County courthouse at 60 Centre Street—the one you see on TV with the long steps and columns. I stood in awe of the place before heading in with the papers. It was the first time—and the only time while I was at the firm—that I felt like a real lawyer.

Other times, Leon would send me out on wild goose chases,

down to the labor and employment office, for example, to try to get information for a client. But most of the time I would have to wait in line several hours and would talk with several different people before coming back empty-handed because the information I needed didn't exist or because whatever people were available that day didn't have access. Even though I'd been handed an impossible task, I'd still end up feeling deflated and worthless after enduring Leon's wrath.

There was a professor from my law school who came to check up on me and ensure that I was learning what I needed to. Once she arrived at the office, I had to put on a good show, as did the partners, so it looked to her like I was actually learning something. I couldn't have said I wasn't learning anything—I needed to graduate. Really, though, we were all pretending. Even she wasn't as concerned about my fit with the firm; I pretty quickly learned that her check-in was mostly just an excuse to take a vacation to New York City.

Even though I didn't receive a valuable education in the field of matrimonial law, that's not to say I didn't learn a lot about what it was like to adopt the lifestyle and career of a successful lawyer. For example, the partners made a lot of money, but I saw right away just how miserable the work made them. Spending sixty to seventy hours a week at something you hated didn't seem like any kind of life to me. *If this is success,* I thought, *I don't want any part of it.* To make matters even worse, Leon and Barry didn't seem to like each other. Small arguments would blow up into huge shouting matches for the entire office to hear. Barry once told me never to start a business with a partner unless it was absolutely necessary. If there is ever a falling out, he said, it's worse than an actual divorce.

After a few weeks at the firm, I started to see why the work itself also made the partners miserable: It was downright depressing to work with the clients, often soon-to-be-divorced husbands and wives fighting over petty things like silverware and pets more than they fought over custody of their own children. After sitting through a few of those fights, it got to the point where I actually started looking forward to my weekends at Applebee's.

The pressure of working every day, not being sure if I was going to be able to take the bar exam, and sleeping in the middle of a living room was beginning to take a toll on me. I started experiencing severe panic attacks on a daily basis.

At first I had no idea what was happening; I'd never experienced anything like a panic attack before. One day, after a long day at the law firm, I got on the subway to head home. Once I got into the crowded car, I made my way toward the door between the train cars and leaned up against it. Suddenly, a rush came over me. My heart started beating very fast, my palms started sweating, I couldn't think straight, and I was having trouble breathing. I bent over and squatted down with my head between my knees. I didn't understand what was going on, and all I could do was pray that it would just end. I stayed in that position until my stop. I slowly got up, pushed my way through the crowded subway car to the open doors, and squeezed my way out. The attack started to subside once I climbed out of the subway tunnel and hit the fresh air. But I was scared and worried about what I had just experienced.

After that, panic attacks became a daily occurrence for me. Usually, they would start around the same time, while I was at the law firm in the afternoon. I didn't seek help, because I had neither the time nor the health insurance to cover the costs of medical attention. I popped ibuprofen like Tic Tacs to keep the attacks under control. I continued to wonder what was wrong with me and just kept telling myself that the externship would soon end and hopefully so would the panic attacks. I just wanted to get away and not have to go back to the law firm. *Is this what living in New York City is all about? Do I not have what it takes to live here?* I was always questioning myself and my decisions.

At long last, my externship was over, and I could graduate from law school. I headed back to Michigan to get my degree. The day of my graduation ceremony, as I sat in my seat, waiting to receive my degree, I felt my palms start to sweat. I knew what was about to happen: I was going to have a severe panic attack. Looking around, everyone else seemed so happy and excited, while I just wanted this attack to subside. I thought of my college graduation when I'd gotten too stoned to remember receiving my diploma. This time, I was able to get myself together in time to walk across the stage, but I wasn't able to enjoy or remember the moment because I was so focused on not losing my shit. Yes, I had graduated from law school. But I was still uncertain and afraid about what might lie ahead. I didn't know whether I would be able to pass the bar or, even more troubling, the character and fitness evaluation. I started to have visions of my criminal record laid out before me, a stern-looking man or woman in a suit with a big red stamp that said *Denied*. Triple B attended the ceremony and told me afterward: "Quite the accomplishment, I would have lost a bet."

I graduated largely in part because of meeting and studying with Brent and Dalton. I am so grateful for their support and camaraderie during law school. I'm not sure I would have graduated without them. Although I wasn't sure what the future had in store for me, both Brent and Dalton eventually became Judges in their respective states.

After graduation, my panic attacks subsided for the most part and

I decided to return to New York City and take the bar exam. It felt like a huge risk, investing all my time and money into the bar when I still didn't know if I would be allowed to be a lawyer, but I had already come this far. And after all, what did I have to lose? I would focus on passing the bar exam first and go from there. To study, most aspiring lawyers sign up for a bar exam course, which costs around $3,000. I thought that was silly. After three years of law school, I had to pay thousands of dollars more just to study for an exam I had thought I was studying for over the past three years? I decided to forgo the course, partly because I didn't have the cash and partly because I thought it didn't really matter if I passed the bar, because I was sure I wouldn't be able to pass the character and fitness evaluation. I signed up for the exam and studied half-heartedly over the next few months.

The exam was held at the Jacob Javits Convention Center, a huge glass building on the banks of the Hudson River. Thousands of wannabe attorneys filed into this huge space that was normally used for expos and conventions. That particular day, the floor was filled with hundreds of tables and chairs. Once everyone took their seats, massive garage doors closed down all around us. When the exam was over, I quickly exited the building to get some air. I knew I had failed, and that was confirmed a few weeks later.

By this time, I was working in New Jersey at LexisNexis, a legal research and publishing company, as a customer support representative. I had moved out of my "room" in Soho and was living in a proper apartment in Hell's Kitchen. The job didn't pay much, and I had to borrow money from my mother sometimes to make ends meet. I would get up three hours early every day and take the train from the Port Authority out to New Jersey for work. It was over an hour-long commute. Even though I did this and relied on the train, I was never once late to work. I knew that trains are unreliable, so I always took the train that was scheduled to arrive an hour and a half early just in case something happened.

I decided to try the bar exam again and actually take the prep course this time. I also quit working at Applebee's so I could focus on studying more. After I took the train home each day, I would walk from the Port Authority to the New York Public Library and study until they closed. On the weekends, I would go to the bar prep class and then study at Starbucks or the library. Neither place was particularly conducive to studying. Starbucks had too much noise and activity, and the New York Public Library wasn't all that quiet, either. More often than not, there were more people in there sleeping and getting kicked out than actually studying. Still, I wasn't going to let myself take the bar exam again without giving it my all, which I hadn't done the first time.

The weekends and long nights paid off. I passed the New York bar exam on my second attempt. Of course, this would still mean nothing if I wasn't able to get through the character and fitness evaluation.

I knew that I had a long history of immoral conduct that would be scrutinized by any reasonable employer or gatekeeper—especially the ones deciding who did or didn't deserve to practice law. But I wasn't that person anymore, not really. I thought back to my high school days selling acid in the bathrooms. Representing myself in court after countless fights had finally led to being arrested for a crime I hadn't committed. Or to Kent State, the day-drinking, the accident, my car wrapped around the telephone pole and the city dark around me. All that time worrying about fulfilling Triple B's prophecy and being a loser my entire life, and yet I'd never let that spark inside me die out, and somewhere along the line I'd turned things around. Now here I was, aiming to better myself and make a decent living. Working my butt off, not just for cash to take to the bar but to save up for study courses, to support myself until I was able to pass the bar and build the life I wanted.

I was terrified that with one single interview, I'd lose everything. But as much as I wanted to think back and beat myself up for every dumb decision I'd ever made, I knew I had to look forward. I had come so far in life already, jumped through so many hoops to be here. And I thought that if I had come this far, why couldn't I go a bit farther? I decided to disclose everything I had ever done wrong to the New York bar, as is required.

Not only did I need to disclose my criminal conduct, but I also had to disclose my juvenile criminal conduct and even minor speeding tickets. Looking at the forms in front of me, I knew it was going to take me some time to amass all of this information. I took the task seriously. If I was going to be honest, I had better really be honest. I flew back to Ohio to each individual police station where I'd been arrested to get certified copies of the police report, my arrest record, and the results of each case. I had to do this for each instance of disorderly conduct, underage drinking, disturbing the peace, speeding tickets, assault, driving under a suspended license, hit and skip, and driving under the influence. I assembled it all and then submitted it to the New York state Bar Committee on Character and Fitness. *Gulp.*

After all the information is submitted, every applicant has to be interviewed by an upstanding member of the bar or officer of the court, like a judge or prosecutor. On the day I was assigned to come in, there were hundreds of us being interviewed. We all sat in a huge room on the twenty-sixth floor in the building for the Committee on

Character and Fitness on Madison Avenue. From there, they called us in ten at a time into another room, where we would actually wait to be interviewed. From within the second room, I could see the applicants getting interviewed through a window on the other side. It seemed that each interview was taking about five minutes or so.

When I was called into the second room, I sat there for quite some time. At least an hour passed, and I grew increasingly nervous. Everyone else was getting called into their respective interviews. I found out later that they were waiting for a "special" prosecutor to interview me.

Finally, I heard my name. I saw that the file with my name on it was covered with all sorts of red markings and notes. I was led over to a woman who introduced herself as a prosecutor. I sat down in front of her and she started going through my file and pulling out papers, barely looking up at me. She sat there, not saying a word, for what seemed like an eternity. It felt like a lifetime was passing by. She read papers and pushed them to the side.

Then she pulled out one paper and focused on it, examining it in great detail. She finally asked me, "I see you recently got caught speeding?"

"Yes," I answered, surprised. "I was late for class in law school and didn't want to miss anything."

She looked into my eyes and said, "How do I know you're not going to make this same mistake again?"

Without thinking, I replied, "Now that I live in New York City, I don't have a car anymore, so I won't be driving."

She continued to thumb through my paperwork. Without looking up at me, she said, "You have quite the file here. Are you going to be an upstanding and honest attorney?"

"Yes, if given the chance."

"Okay then," she said, signing a paper. "You're all set. Congratulations."

It was as if a weight had been lifted off my shoulders. I couldn't think or breathe, but it wasn't because of a panic attack. I was stunned—and proud. I was in! I had passed the character and fitness evaluation. The next day, I was sworn in as a lawyer and officer of the court at the historic First Judicial Department of the Appellate Division of the Supreme Court building: I, Kyle Victor Robinson, who had taken six years to graduate high school, gone to drug rehab, been arrested countless times, almost failed out of college, and been written off as a loser, was a licensed New York attorney!

Once I had been sworn in as a licensed attorney, I thought I'd try my hand at actually practicing law. In the weeks following my character evaluation, I probably applied for over one hundred jobs and received either polite rejections or silence. I did get an interview or two but never heard back. At first, I kept all my rejection letters, as if I was going to use them as motivation to get a law job. But they quickly started piling up.

Though I was eager to find a job, I wasn't as affected by the rejections as I might have been. After my experience at my externship, watching how the work required to make a firm successful had also drained the life out of two incredibly wealthy men, I wasn't even really sure if I wanted to practice law. On the other hand, that might have been something I told myself to ease the pain of not being able to find a job practicing law. Because I did want a job, even if only for the validation. It's what I had gone to school for, after all. But I was learning that there were many licensed attorneys in New York, and the degree wasn't all that mattered. I didn't have the experience or the grades. On top of that, the legal market was in the toilet.

Even though I couldn't find a job practicing law, I would settle for a job in the city that paid more than what I was currently making as a customer support representative in Jersey. So I expanded the scope of my search and started applying to positions where a law degree was "preferred." Eventually I was hired as an account executive selling legal services and electronic discovery equipment for lawyers at a company based in downtown Manhattan. No more train rides out to New Jersey for me!

The company worked like this: Basically, law firms would give us boxes and boxes of legal papers, which we would condense down to a single disc. My job was to go from law firm to law firm, picking up and dropping off boxes. In the meantime, I made cold calls to firms pitching our services. It was a valuable service to lawyers; condensing those files took hours and hours of work. I didn't particularly like the job, and it didn't fulfill me, but at least I was a little more content. I was working in the city and was able to make a living.

What I really wanted, I realized, was not just something steady that would pay my bills, but something that would challenge me and allow me to grow as a person. So as I trekked across Manhattan from firm to firm, dialing up the landline for call after all, I also continued my job search. Eventually I landed an interview with an online continuing legal education company. Attorneys have to take courses to maintain their license, and this company provided such courses through their website. It seemed like a good fit for me. The company had an award-winning culture, and they seemed to be excited about me as a potential employee. I originally applied to be a sales associate. However, after I interviewed, it was clear to them I'd be more of an asset talking to attorneys and helping develop and facilitate legal education programs. Therefore, I was brought on as a program attorney. When I received the offer, it was a pay cut from what I was currently making, but I didn't care because I was more concerned about working in a great environment, no longer in sales, and actually using my degree.

Although the company wasn't a start-up, it had a start-up atmosphere. There were fewer than twenty employees. Everyone was young, including the president and CEO (he was the same age as me), and we were all crammed into small offices, working together to create online content in a building in the financial district downtown on the nineteenth floor. My desk was in an office in the back, which I shared with three other employees.

This job was like no other I'd had. It gave me the freedom to do it how I wanted to without a boss micromanaging me. I worked in an atmosphere where my bosses believed in me, encouraged me to do good things, and actually wanted to see me succeed. In fact, the president of the company, Gary, would go on to become one of my best friends, my mentor, and somebody who showed me that I was capable of much more than I thought I was.

I no longer dreaded getting up in the morning to go to work. My panic attacks were a thing of the past. I looked forward to seeing everyone at the office. I was actually creating something meaningful, performing a job I was qualified to perform. I was growing confident in my abilities. Nobody was breathing down my neck, telling me what to do and how to do it, and I didn't have the stress of a sales quota to meet. Although my primary job was to create legal content for the company, I was permitted to do so much more.

The best part of the job was my opportunity to do non-work-related things. For example, employees were allowed and even encouraged to address the company at the morning meeting on whatever they liked, and I took full advantage. My presentations tended to focus on health, wellness, and personal development. At one point, I gave a presentation titled "Kyle's Kool-Aid: Twelve Secrets to Happiness." These were ideals I aspire to live up to:

1) Everyone deserves a second chance;
2) Say sorry even when it's not your fault;
3) Be thankful;
4) Keep an open mind;
5) Chase your fear;
6) The past does not predict the future;
7) Take 100% responsibility for your life;
8) Laugh;
9) Keep positive people around you;
10) Believe in and be yourself;
11) Make your bed every morning; and
12) Above all, love yourself and be kind to others.

It was the first opportunity I'd ever had to share my story and where I had come from. Although I didn't go into much detail, I did vaguely reference some of my struggles. I presented a workshop on goals, which involved everyone writing down their goals and how they would achieve them. I also had an opportunity to lead a workshop on optimism and seeing the brighter side of things.

They might have just been small presentations, but for me they represented something so much greater. I had spent so much time, it felt, ceding control—to Triple B, to the urge to party, or the need to seek approval from my peers, to the belief that I would never amount to anything. But now I was actually developing and creating my life, instead of letting it create me. Young Kyle could have never imagined this life, thriving in New York City and sharing his story with others, offering his own tips for how to live, find happiness and peace. These presentations would even inspire me to do a few speaking engagements outside of the company, sharing my story of arrests and failing out of school with kids in foster care or after-school programs. Even now, those presentations always get a good reception, and they always make me feel like I'm making a difference.

In time, I was also given a supervisory role, which I'd never had before at any other job. I directly supervised the law student interns we hired and was also involved in the employee hiring and interview process. I thought I had finally made it and I would never leave this place. I worked long hours and came in on the weekends. Having someone actually believe in me and in my abilities was a life-changing confidence booster. It was as if everything I had dreamed of was coming to fruition. For the first time in my life, I had friends who wanted the best for me and were rooting for me. I had never known what that was like before. There were two individuals in particular who shaped me during that time: Gary and Joseph. If it weren't for their guidance, friendship, and mentoring, I wouldn't have eventually found my true voice or my authentic self.

Joseph was the company's video producer, and he was responsible for all the filming, editing, and audio aspects of our material. I worked very closely with him to develop our legal programs and got to know him very well. Joseph had a number of unique abilities that made him an extraordinary human being, many of which anyone would be able to see within five minutes of meeting him. Three come to mind immediately.

First, he was a very hard worker. I don't mean in the sense that he'd work all day and all night to get a job done. He'd do that, too, but he'd also make sure the job was done exactly right. Time and time again, I witnessed him go back over a particular program or video setup just to get it perfect. If it took extra hours, or even if the project needed to be done over again from scratch, that's what he'd do. Many people won't do that; Joseph would not only do it, he'd do it without complaint.

Second, Joseph was passionate about feminism and women's rights, more so than anyone else I'd ever met. His beliefs gave me a deeper awareness of the atrocities and horrors related to sexism all around me. I began to see the world in a different way because of him. Every time he talked about feminism, I could see the passion in his eyes and hear it in his voice. He truly made a difference—I am living proof.

Finally, this attribute is the one I believe makes Joseph so special and is the reason he is one of the most amazing people I've met: simply put, he never judged people or situations. That is, he treated everyone with respect no matter who they were or how they looked. He gave them the benefit of the doubt every time. This attribute is one I most wanted to possess, and he had it. Years later, when my sister and I would catch each other judging people or situations, we would always say, "What would Joseph do?" I really do try to think about what Joseph would do or think in certain situations, and I then know how to act. This nonjudgmental approach is what makes Joseph, Joseph.

Gary, the president of the company, had a confidence I craved. Like me, Gary was a licensed attorney in New York but had decided not to practice. He wanted something more out of life and had the passion and drive to go after it. He's the one who sparked something in me that pushed me to achieve greater things. Like Joseph, Gary possessed qualities that I truly admired.

First of all, he was eager to learn. Gary always said, "Teaching is the best form of learning." Basically, if you want to learn something very well, simply explain it to someone else. That's one of the reasons why I presented a program on happiness, optimism, and goals to the company—because I wanted to learn more about them myself. Gary was an avid reader, and he inspired me to get my hands on as many books as possible. Specifically Gary loved entrepreneurship books and recommended *Good to Great* by Jim Collins and *Find Your Why* by Simon Sinek. Because of Gary's passion for books I was inspired to continue reading and I discovered books that had a huge impact on the way I live my life and how I think, such as *The Alchemist* by Paulo Coelho, *The Obstacle is the Way* by Ryan Holiday, and *Tuesdays with Morrie* by Mitch Albom. Gary's attitude toward learning came from a desire to become a better person, which is something I've always craved as well. That's one reason why we got along so well.

Second, Gary wasn't afraid to speak his mind. This can be both negative and positive. But above all else, I always knew where I stood with Gary. If he didn't like something someone did or if he didn't think much of it, he would let them know. After I did my first presentation on optimism for the company, I was feeling down because I felt it hadn't gone well and I could have done better. I went into Gary's office and asked him what he thought. I was searching for something positive, but he informed me that it wasn't the best presentation he had seen. He didn't think much of my public speaking skills, and he let me know I could do much better. I left his office feeling a little deflated, but it inspired me to try harder. To help me out, Gary signed me up for a public speaking class offered at New York University. I kept doing presentations for the office, getting better, and not giving up. However, at the same time, Gary could buoy me up, encourage me, and make me feel good about my work, who I was, and where I was heading in life. He always encouraged me to think outside the box, so to speak.

Finally, Gary wasn't afraid to take risks. He would try anything to see what results were possible. We started a business venture together while I was working with him—a start-up school for start-up businesses—and it was a complete disaster. But he didn't see it as a failure. He was willing to take risks no matter what other people thought. He simply didn't care. I wanted that ability—I still do.

I really got to know Gary well when we trained to run a marathon together. I had started running on a regular basis in law school, a hobby my sister had initially sparked. Gary renewed my passion for running. He had never run a marathon before, and I was ready for another one, so we signed up for the Philadelphia Marathon and trained together. When you train for that sort of race with someone, you spend a lot of time together. We both lived in Brooklyn at the time, I in Crown Heights, and he in Park Slope. I would run over to his house on the weekends, and we would go for our long runs through the city streets. It was like a video game avoiding cabs, people, and open doors. Since we worked together, we would run home from work, too.

Even though running took up a lot of my time, I was more focused on work and was being more productive than ever. But there was still something inside of me yearning for more. I admired and respected Joseph and Gary, and liked working for them. But at the end of the day, I was working for someone else when what I really needed, I started to realize, was to work for myself. I couldn't shake the itch for freedom, the ability to get up in the morning and do exactly what I wanted to do. No matter how much I respected my bosses, something still rubbed me wrong about working my butt off for someone else's company. If I wanted to work that hard, it should have been for myself and for something I was passionate about.

Other employees who had, like me, made it to the top of the company had asked for a piece of the company, and Gary had always said no. I never asked—I wasn't really made to be a "company man," and I wanted to find my own way, to start something of my own. Law school had taught me that I was just as smart and capable as my peers; as much as I respected Gary, I thought I was capable of building something successful just like he had built his company. *His* company.

By the time I started having these doubts, there were new employees at the company by then who had more "fire" than I did at the time. They were a better fit for my role than I was, and I was ready to step aside and let them lead. After a lot of deliberation, I decided that I needed to move on from Gary's company and this job that I loved so much.

So my time in New York came to an end. I had been there almost five years, and I wasn't the same insecure person I had been when I arrived. I'd look out the window from the nineteenth floor down on Broadway in downtown Manhattan and see waves of people walking. To me, they looked carefree, and most importantly, they weren't chained to a desk. I wondered why they didn't have jobs, or if they did, what they did that made them enough money to pay their pricey New York rent and gave them such freedom to be out in the middle of the day. I understood they all had their own stories and problems to deal with, but I fantasized about their all being free and doing whatever they wanted, and I wanted that same freedom outside of an office.

Gary and I mutually agreed it was time for me to move on from the company—so he let me go to enable me to receive unemployment benefits. Leaving was bittersweet. At the time, I thought that perhaps New York City had gotten the best of me, because I hadn't been there that long, but the honest truth is that I needed different experiences in my life to grow. I had many valuable experiences in New York that have become part of who I am and shaped me as a person—a better person. Life just had something different in store for me, and I needed to find out what that was. After almost five years, I decided to move back to Ohio without a job or any job prospects.

CHAPTER 6

Going Ultra

A few months before my move back to Ohio, I was packing up boxes when I glanced toward the full-length mirror leaning up against the wall in my studio apartment in Crown Heights. The person looking back at me was an overweight, out-of-shape guy with a promising double chin. Somehow I had ballooned to over two hundred pounds, and I was back to my heaviest weight when I was doing construction with Carl right out of college.

When I was a kid and a teenager, I never really had a problem with my weight. I certainly never considered myself fat. I had a great metabolism and was very active in sports, running around the neighborhood, and skateboarding. It wasn't until I hit college that I started putting on a few pounds. In college, I drank too much, didn't exercise, and ate whatever I wanted, whenever I wanted. Working at Swensons didn't help either; I had too many double cheeseburgers every shift. After college, I didn't change my diet too much. I didn't think I was fat; I just thought I had to shed a few pounds. It was nothing to be concerned about for me. The truth was, I was clinically obese. When I moved out to San Francisco, I was more active and the pounds came off without me even trying, though I was still overweight. Then, when I was in law school, I put the weight back on. Studying constantly, a sedentary lifestyle, and a lack of exercise didn't exactly do wonders for my health. When I moved out to New York City, I put on even more weight because I was working constantly, stressing out, not exercising, going out drinking, and still eating whatever I wanted. Even when I was running and training for the marathons, I was still eating junk food right after the runs. I used the training runs as an excuse to go overboard on the sweets and unhealthy foods. So when I saw myself in the mirror that day, I knew this was an issue I needed to address before I moved back to Ohio.

To be honest, I didn't know where to start. I had dabbled in running a little bit in San Francisco and in law school and had already run two marathons: the New York City Marathon with my sister in 2010 and the Philadelphia Marathon in 2012 with Gary. Those were real achievements, and I was proud of them. But I used these two marathons to "prove" to myself that I was in shape. In reality, they just enabled me to continue lying to myself. I ran both of those races out of shape with dismal times. Deep down, I knew I could have done better. On that life-changing morning, the mirror didn't lie.

I started running because I wanted to get in shape and because I loved the feeling of being outdoors, exploring, and challenging myself. Running is good exercise, but it didn't necessarily mean I was going to lose weight. After I ran my first two marathons, I didn't understand why I wasn't losing any weight. In fact, I had gained weight.

The night of the mirror incident, after I ate a few frozen chicken burritos and several chocolate chip cookies crushed up in a bowl with milk that I ate like cereal, I watched a documentary titled *Forks over Knives*. This documentary advocated a low-fat, whole-foods, plant-based diet. I ate up everything the movie said, both literally and figuratively. People featured in the movie had lost weight and gotten healthy almost instantly after adopting a plant-based diet. I was so moved by the movie, I quit eating meat that very night. When I coupled a meatless diet with running, the weight came off even when I wasn't trying to lose it.

That summer, I packed up a rented minivan and headed west to Columbus, Ohio, where my sister lived. I had never lived in Columbus, even though it was two hours south of my hometown, Cuyahoga Falls. I didn't want to move back to Cuyahoga Falls because it had too many bad influences and bad memories for me. Plus, I wanted to experience something different. For the fifth time in my life, I rented an apartment sight unseen and moved without a source of income.

When I arrived, I went crazy applying for jobs, but nothing came to fruition. I wanted something more than working at Applebee's; I was a licensed attorney for goodness' sake! I was starting to become depressed and scared that I had made a huge mistake. I was on the verge of running out of my unemployment benefits. I felt worthless. I had literally no income and bills were piling up daily.

Finally, I received a job offer as a legal recruiter. My job involved identifying law firms who were hiring and then finding and securing the appropriate, qualified, candidate to fill these specific office vacancies. Typically, these positions were temporary and involved mostly administrative work. Occasionally, I would fill a long-term position for an attorney. I got paid a commission based on the length of the positions I filled—long-term positions were the money makers, but rare.

It was tough because there was a lot of turnover in the industry and finding a strong candidate was difficult. There was a term I heard my boss toss around the office: "temporary workers are temporary for a reason." Hearing that, I knew he had no respect for his work or for the people we were helping. It was a job with a miserable cutthroat environment that I would soon come to despise.

My boss lived in Minnesota, but my direct report was in the Columbus office. He was the opposite of Gary in that he didn't know how to be a manager or a boss. He would constantly put me down or give me assignments that he didn't want to do himself, just to try to control me. He was always talking bad about our boss in Minnesota, as well as everyone else, so I could only imagine what he was saying to everyone else about me. The whole experience was the opposite of what I'd gotten used to at Gary's company. I'm sure I wasn't the best employee because I was so used to having the freedom to make my own decision, but even so, I knew how to play the game and could have been a savvy salesperson if I'd wanted to. But the toxic environment was too much. It paid the bills, but it didn't make me feel good about myself when I went home at the end of the day.

As it turned out, it was probably a good thing I'd landed a job that I hated so much because it was while I was working there that I decided to start my own continuing legal education company, like the one I had worked at with Gary. I thought, *If Gary can be successful with this, why couldn't I?* I knew the business very well, and it didn't take much capital to get started, which was appealing because I didn't have any money and nothing to lose.

After work each day, I went straight to the library to get my new business venture off the ground. I had no idea how to make a website so I watched hours upon hours of YouTube videos that taught me how to create a paid membership-based website. After weeks of trial and error, I got a rudimentary, but decent, working website up.

Additionally, the "Business Organizations" and "Tax" classes I'd liked so much in law school became invaluable. I scoured my notes for information that helped me get set up as a legitimate entity in Ohio. Once that was up and running, I needed legal course content for attorneys to take. I had done a few programs while I worked with Gary, so I decided that because I was a lawyer, I could just record my own content for the time being. Again, I used my law school outlines and textbooks to create and record my first courses. Once I got going, I could recruit other attorneys to provide additional content.

The next step was going through the process of getting the courses accredited in Ohio so attorneys would be able to receive credit for them. Once the courses were approved, I put them live on my website and waited. Within an hour, I got my first sale. *Holy shit!* I thought. I wasn't even advertising yet. Hell, I wasn't even really ready yet. I had a sale though, a sale from something I had created out of nothing. It was an amazing feeling, and it only reinforced my belief that I could make this work. Then I thought, *If this first program is successful, why don't I expand to other states?* So that's what I did.

After four months as a legal recruiter, I quit and focused solely on my own business. I probably didn't quit in the most professional way. I wrote my boss in Minnesota an email about how I couldn't work in this toxic environment anymore. Immediately after sending the email to my boss, I told one of my work colleagues, whom I didn't get along with, that I was going to go grab a quick cup of coffee down the street—and I never came back.

I also didn't tell Gary, at first, about starting my own business. I thought he might be upset that I was "stealing" his idea. I got a call from him one day and he didn't seem happy, and I knew the jig was up. He told me that he just wished he hadn't heard about it from someone else. He also told me something I'll never forget:

"I can't be angry or upset with you because that would speak more to insecurities about me and my company. I wish you all the best." So with his blessing and our friendship still intact, I was on my way with this new venture.

My lease was up in Columbus and I needed to plot out my next move. My sister had her own life and friends in Columbus, and I didn't really feel a part of it. Also, I felt I had to move on. As fate would have it, Triple B and Mom had just bought a retirement cabin in rural Lancaster, Ohio, about fifty miles south of Columbus. They bought the place before they were ready to move because the interest rates were so low at the time. Mom also still had a few months before she was able to retire and move. Mom asked if I wanted to live in the cabin and watch over it before they moved in. Mom loved the idea of me moving into the cabin, thinking it would bring me and Triple B closer, but it didn't, and I shouldn't have accepted their offer without thinking it over more. Although this arrangement would benefit me greatly. I would live rent-free and work on my business. And that's exactly what I did. I spent my mornings running and my afternoons recording content for my website. Being basically in the middle of nowhere and with no distractions or bad influences, I was able to read a lot, get in physical shape, and grow my business exponentially. The solitude was nice and allowed me to learn a lot about myself—specifically about how I was raised. I started to question some things internally. However, I was lonely and missed social interactions.

The days of Triple B and Mom moving to the cabin were fast approaching and I needed to move out. Before they moved in, Mom called and asked me to come help Triple B move their stuff into a storage unit because the new owners were moving in the next day into their Cuyahoga Falls home and they didn't have anyone else to help them. I obliged because they let me live in the cabin rent free. I spent the entire day hauling their furniture into a moving truck and didn't receive any thanks or appreciation in response. The last time I'd seen Triple B before that was the previous Thanksgiving, when he'd spent most of the time complaining and eventually yelling at my sister's sons, rambunctious toddlers who had the gall to play with their toys at the dinner table. I felt pretty done, with Triple B at least, and I didn't want to be around when they came into town.

Since I moved out of Mom and Triple B's house years ago for college, I only talked to him when it was absolutely necessary. The worst was on birthdays or holidays when Mom would call and then, after we'd been talking for a while, try to give the phone to Triple B. "Your father is here, do you want to talk to him?" she'd ask, and then put him on without waiting for an answer. I would cringe and start to get angry. *My father.* I didn't have a thing to say to him—at least nothing that wouldn't end up with the two of us yelling and my mother weeping on the other end. I didn't understand how or why she was still trying to make this relationship happen, but I also didn't want to upset her. Instead, Triple B and I would make stilted conversation for about ten seconds or so, then we'd hang up or he'd hand the phone back to Mom.

Fortunately, Brad had just moved back from San Francisco to Cleveland and was working in the solar business. Specifically, he was selling solar panels for homes over the phone across the county. He needed some part-time help and asked if I was interested. Because my business wasn't quite generating enough money for me to live and

I needed to get out of the cabin, I decided I would move to Cleveland and help Brad while I continued to grow my own business.

In Cleveland, I spent a lot of time alone. I didn't really hang out with Brad or other friends because they spent most of their time drinking and smoking weed. I had no choice but to focus on my business, and it grew as a result. It grew so much I didn't need to work with Brad anymore.

My business was finally booming and I also had more time, finally, to focus on myself. I started a regular meditation practice at this time, because so many people I admired swore by it. It quieted my mind and helped me gain clarity and focus, both of which I needed. Also, it was a good tool to keep panic attacks at bay. At this time, I started to gravitate toward a new group of friends, too: runners. I wanted to stay fit and be around people who would push my limits. I joined a local running group and slowly stopped spending time with my old friends. Brad and I naturally grew apart.

After a while, we had a solid group of four runners—me, PJ, Chris, and Eric, who we all called Baby because he was the youngest by nearly fifteen years—running together a few days a week. Chris and PJ actually were at Kent State at the same time I was, though I'd never met them there. PJ was a bartender at one of the local spots, so we almost definitely interacted. Like me, Chris and PJ grew up with a difficult family situation, but unlike me, they seemed to make it through their teenage years and young adulthood without all the chaos. Still, it made me feel like I'd found a group that finally understood me. A group formed around a healthy habit rather than unhealthy ones.

We created a group called the Cleveland Explorers Club and started meeting at 5:30 a.m. to go on runs exploring the city. We all had to pay "dues" each week—just a couple of bucks to keep us accountable. Anyone who was late had to pay an extra fifty cents, and if you didn't show up, you owed a dollar. Pretty quickly, we started pushing each other to run faster and farther.

As I got more and more into running, I spent a lot of time reading about the subject, especially ultramarathon runners. There was something about ultrarunning that was exciting and fascinating. It seemed like a challenge of the mind and body. I liked the idea of being stripped down to nothing emotionally and seeing what I was really capable of. When my body is telling me to quit at mile forty because I feel like my legs or body can't move, it's my mind that I use to convince me otherwise—if I'm strong enough to convince myself—and that's what makes ultramarathon running the ultimate mental challenge. I run because I like to push my own boundaries, see what's on the other side of fear, and know what I'm truly capable of. I felt that if I could run a hundred miles without stopping, there wasn't anything in this world I couldn't do. At the same time, I'm sure my somewhat addictive personality liked the idea of the races and running. It was something I could be obsessed with that had a—mostly—positive impact.

I was also inspired by Dean Karnazes's book *Ultramarathon Man* and Christopher McDougall's book *Born to Run*, both of which are about the sport of ultrarunning.

In addition, I discovered that some of the best ultrarunners don't eat meat. I read Scott Jurek's book *Eat and Run* and Rich Roll's book *Finding Ultra*. They're both ultra-endurance athletes who are also vegan. Scott Jurek was arguably one of the best ultrarunners ever. He has won the most prestigious ultramarathon in the United States, the Western States 100, seven times in a row. Rich Roll is a recovering alcoholic who got into races later in life. When Rich was in his forties, he completed the Epic 5—five ultra-ironman-distances in less than a week. Both of these guys inspired me because there is nothing sensational about them besides their athletic endurance achievements, so I was able to relate and believe I was capable of more. They are normal humans who just happened to dedicate themselves to something and made it work. If they could do it, I thought, so could I.

I was getting in better shape and dropped from 200 pounds to 155 pounds. Inspired by the books I had read and ready for my next challenge, I signed up for an ultramarathon in Washington, DC—the North Face Endurance Challenge fifty-mile trail race—on June 6, 2014. I fully intended to dedicate my mind and body to accomplishing this goal. I needed to see what I was capable of.

I'm not the fastest runner, and I didn't run track in high school or college. I did run in junior high though, where I did the hurdles, the eight-hundred-meter race, and the long jump, and I was pretty good at all of them. So with this extensive running background, I was ready to tackle the ultra-marathon.

Now I just needed a plan. And not only did I need a plan, but I needed to follow through with it. I researched online training programs for a fifty-mile race. I also knew that nutrition was a big part of training, and I was determined to use my new secret of plant power for the race.

I had never done a trail race, let alone a fifty-miler, and I didn't know what to expect. I decided to volunteer at another fifty-miler to see what I was going to be in for. The North Face holds trail races throughout the year and throughout the world, so finding one of their races to volunteer at wasn't difficult. I found one in Bear Mountain,

New York, which was about an hour north of New York City. My job was to help runners refuel at an aid station about twenty-two miles in.

Volunteering at the race turned out to provide crucial information. As runners came into the aid station, grabbed a quick bite, and filled their hydration packs as fast as they could, I soaked up information like a sponge. I made sure to take notice of what they were wearing, how they ate, how much time they spent at the aid station, and even how they ran. This was all foreign to me, and I fell in love with it instantly. I knew I wanted to experience being on the other side of the aid station.

During the race, I saw the fastest trail runners in the world and others who were basically just walking. Some runners even had pacers to keep them company and encourage them.

If I were going to attempt something this epic, I was going to need to have someone just as epic as a pacer.

Enter Joseph from my old company in NYC.

Joseph was an accomplished marathon runner, and I knew I would benefit so much from his company and experience during the race.

In the days leading up to the race, I was confident that I had done everything in my power to prepare as much as possible. I drove to Algonkian Regional Park in Sterling, Virginia—where the race would actually take place—a day early to check things out and get settled in. I went down to the starting line and watched the volunteers setting up tents and preparing for the next day's event. I picked Joseph up from the train station, and we went to an information session in Georgetown for a pre-race report and talk being held by the race organizers. I needed to get as much information as possible.

When we arrived, though, I was surprised by how few people were there. The race was the next day, and there were thousands signed up to run different distances, the marathon, 50K, relay team, or 50 miler. The information was interesting but not crucial. They let us know how our "bibs" were going to be marked by officials as we made our way through the various loops around the course. Still, it was helpful from a mental aspect to know what to expect the next day so I wasn't left wondering and I felt more prepared.

After the meeting, I dropped Joseph off at the hotel. I wouldn't see him again until mile thirty during the race, where he would start running with me. I had an early dinner and tried to get some sleep. I needed to be up for a five a.m. race start.

The next morning, the hotel gave me a three a.m. wake-up call, and I rolled out of bed excited. I was pleasantly surprised that I had actually gotten a good night's sleep, considering what was ahead of me. I had already laid all of my clothes and supplies out the night before, so now I donned my gray shorts and blue shirt. I pinned my race bib on my shorts. I filled my handheld water bottle with a mix of grape Gatorade and water. Then I stuffed as many gels in the available pockets as I could. For breakfast, I feasted on a banana and an everything bagel with almond butter. The race was only about four miles from my hotel, but I headed down early because I knew my nerves would send me to the port-a-potty a few times. I just wanted to get this thing going. I had dedicated almost six months of my life to preparing for this moment, and now it was here.

This race start was divided into different "waves" and times, so as to not clog up the trail with all the runners in the first few miles of the race. Usually, the faster runners, or "elites," are in the first wave. Ultrarunning is one of the few sports where amateurs are able to compete toe-to-toe with the elites, and though I was originally selected to be in wave two, I had the option of moving up to wave one. I wanted a good start and to know what it felt like to start a race with the fastest runners, so I went with wave one.

Dean Karnazes, the Ultramarathon Man, was there to start us off, but he wasn't running the race. Dean raised the starter pistol toward the sky, fired, and we were off. It was still dark out, and most of the runners wore headlamps. The sea of headlamps bobbing up and down through the forest was strange and an awe-inspiring sight. As soon as the race started, a group of four runners sprinted out from the first wave in front of everyone. *There's no way they can keep up that pace*, I thought. It was probably just a mind game on their end, which I suppose is something of a strategy.

I knew this was going to be a long day and there was no need to go out guns blazing. I stayed with the second group of the first wave, right behind the lead sprinters. In the first few miles, we ran along the edge of a pond where there was a thin layer of mist resting on top. At that moment, I didn't want to be anywhere else. I had this feeling of belonging, and I didn't want it to go away. All of these runners were here to run together in the woods. It was one of the best feelings in my life, and at that moment, I knew ultrarunning was for me.

The group I was running with stuck together for the first ten or so miles. We saw the sun come up together as we followed each other along the single-track trail. As we ran, we would help each other out, and if there was a log or rock in the way, I'd hear the pack leader yell, "*Log!*" I had never experienced this type of camaraderie in a race before. It wasn't about competition; it was about the experience and making sure everyone finished the race. We had all done the training, and we were all in this together. We took turns leading the group, and I had my own chance to yell out "*Log!*" a few times. It felt good to keep tempo with a group.

Everything seemed to be going well—and then my first spot of trouble hit. Around mile eight, there was a small creek we were supposed to run though. As we approached the water, we all had to stop to examine the situation. There was a huge tree that was blocking our path, and it was difficult to determine exactly how we were going to navigate it. Knowing that this was a race, I wanted to get by it as quickly as possible, so I decided to jump over it. I landed hard on my right leg, and I knew something didn't feel right.

When I was a teenager, I tore my ACL while playing backyard football. I never had surgery to fix it, just physical rehab. Now I had reinjured that knee. It hurt and was bruised, but I was determined to go on. I hadn't trained this hard to give up now. I took a few Tylenol and tried to push the pain out of my mind. I couldn't quit anyhow, not with Joseph waiting for me.

I managed to stay with the original group I had started with until mile thirteen. At that point, some of them fell behind and a few pulled ahead. By then, the sun was high above us, and it was getting warmer. I still felt great but knew there was a long way to go. There was also a lot of talking going on between the runners, and I wasn't in the mood to talk—I needed as much energy for running as possible. Although, it was nice to listen to others' conversations.

As we headed into one of the checkpoints, Great Falls, around mile fifteen, there was an official shouting out what place everyone was currently in. As I passed him, he screamed, "Twelfth place, keep it up." I was floored. I knew it was still early in the race, but I was ecstatic and a smile came across my face. *I can do this. I can do really well*, I thought.

Right at Great Falls was an aid station with drop bags, and I saw two runners ahead of me stop. I passed them, climbing to tenth place in the race. It was time to put my head down and focus on meeting up with Joseph.

By the time I reached him, I was still in the top fifteen or so, but I was hurting. He started running and clearly assumed we would be going much faster than I was going. Also, I saw a few elite runners who went out with the first group sitting down at the aid station. I thought it was weird that I had caught up with them. I later learned that they ended up dropping out. I used it as motivation to keep going.

Eventually, the heat, my exhaustion, and my lack of experience got the best of me. I started walking and slipped out of the top fifteen. By then, I didn't really care. I just wanted the race to be over.

The last thirteen miles were the hardest miles I had ever run. I ran out of fluids, and it got to the point where my urine was very dark—not a good sign. Then my knee really started hurting, and I had to question whether I could complete the race. I fell four times but took more Tylenol and kept moving. My body wasn't prepared for this heat, and it was hard to stay hydrated.

In the last ten miles, I was passed seven times. I managed to run the last few miles and ended up in twenty-fourth place. I was in the top twenty-five and had finished in under nine hours! Not bad for my first fifty-mile trail race. There were many times when I could have quit and wanted to quit, but because of Joseph, my training, and my mental toughness, I made it.

The feeling of finishing that trail race in the top twenty-five made me ecstatic. It boosted my confidence to no end. A big part of that confidence came from knowing that this wasn't just a local trail race. This was put on by the North Face and had brought in some elite athletes. Now, all I wanted to do was run trail races and be around the trail-running tribe constantly. All of my training and meatless diet had paid off. If I could dial both of those in even more, I was sure that the sky was the limit of what I was capable of.

My new friends in the Cleveland Explorers Club loved running, no doubt, but they didn't live and breathe ultra-running like I craved. I wanted to challenge myself not only physically, but also mentally. I wanted to become everything I knew I was capable of. I was grateful for the friendship, but I was still convinced I wasn't going to find what I was searching for in Ohio. All the best trail races and runners were out west, and I felt myself being pulled hard in that direction. But first, I would need a van.

CHAPTER 7

Home Is Where I Park It

Around two in the morning, I pulled into a rest stop to get some shut eye in the van for the first time. My eyes felt tired and bleary from staring out at the road for so long, and my brain was foggy from trying to keep myself awake. *Where am I again?* I thought as I looked out through the mosquito-covered windshield to see the moon and a few stars scattered through the clear night sky above. The answer seemed too strange to be true: I was somewhere in Wisconsin, en route from Cleveland to Washington State to meet some people I'd spoken to over email about volunteering for an ultramarathon trail race. It sounded a bit crazy when you put it that way. But it was the truth.

It was a warm night—close to eighty degrees—and the rest stop was surprisingly packed with weary travelers. Sometimes I would see semi-trucks lined up on the sides of the on-ramp and exit ramp to the rest stop—as was the case this night. As I pulled into the parking lot, I searched the lot for a good spot, as I didn't want to park right under a light post or too close to the busy building, where I would hear people coming in and out of the bathroom. I quickly learned that the prime sleeping spots are at the very end of a rest area exit. Although I would hear cars driving in and out or the sound of semi-truck engines running, eventually they would soon become white noise to me when I was trying to get some shut eye. I was lucky enough to grab one of those coveted spots when I saw a green Jeep pulling out. After parking, I grabbed my Dopp kit, locked up the van, and headed to the bathroom to brush my teeth.

Brushing my teeth in a rest stop as the guy to the left of me was taking a leak was an odd experience, as was having strangers coming and leaving as I was going through my nightly routine.

That night, I met a guy in his early twenties with long black hair and a poor excuse for a mustache towing a cartful of kittens. He was in the bathroom cleaning out one of the cats' cages.

"Where ya heading?" he asked me.

I looked up, removed the toothbrush out of my mouth, spat a mouthful of toothpaste foam in the sink, and said, "Washington State. You?"

"I'm from Wisconsin, and I gotta get these cats to my girlfriend in San Diego. You'd be surprised how much they shit on the drive." This was exactly what I wanted to hear as I was brushing my teeth. He continued, clearly wanting to have a conversation at two in the morning in a rest stop bathroom. "Washington State, huh? That's a hell of a drive," he said, hoping I'd say something in return.

I just nodded and started to pack up my things. "Good luck," I said, leaving the bathroom. As I headed toward my van for the night, I thought again, *What the hell am I doing?*

I had a tough time trying to sleep that first night, thanks to the noise from the semi-trucks. Their engines ran all night, even when stopped, and I could hear the drivers entering and exiting the rest stops. Their engines weren't white noise to me yet, and I wasn't fully accustomed to sleeping in the van.

The next day, as I put in more windshield time, I saw North Dakota: its wheat fields, cattle ranches, and strip malls. In Montana, the sky seemed to go on forever, as did the state itself. I saw a few miles of Idaho, and then, finally, I was in Washington State.

I was getting close to my destination, but there was a slight hiccup: I hadn't heard from the race volunteer coordinators in a few days, even after repeated attempts to contact them. I wasn't alarmed, because I knew there wasn't any cell reception on the mountain, but I wasn't sure where exactly to meet them. They were moving all over the mountain, and although we had agreed to meet at Elk Pass, there was also a possibility that they either hadn't arrived yet or that they had arrived and had already left.

As I got closer to Randle, lush evergreens covered the landscape on either side of the two-lane highway. The shops, strip malls, and gas stations gave way to trees, mountains, cabins, and wildlife. As the environment around me turned greener and greener, the signal on my cell phone got weaker and weaker.

I drove through the city of Packwood, which is east of Randle, and stopped at a gas station to fill up and get some beer, so as to not show up empty-handed. As I left the gas station and headed on toward Randle, suddenly, the RV in front of me slammed on its brakes. I came within inches of hitting the bikes attached to its rear bumper. I looked ahead and quickly saw the reason for the abrupt stop. A majestic dark-brown elk was crossing the road without a care in the world.

You're not in Ohio anymore, Kyle.

I finally entered Randle and passed the junior high school on my right. That's where the race was going to finish and where our headquarters were.

Randle was a small town, consisting of three restaurants, a grocery store, the junior high school, the high school, a public library, and a campground. Luckily, I had cell reception in Randle, so I entered the coordinates for Elk Pass that Paul had given me and headed up 131 for our rendezvous.

Although Elk Pass was only about twenty-five miles from Randle, it took over forty-five minutes to drive there. At 6,700 feet above sea level, the road started to get sketchy. There were several potholes and washouts. The van was not made for this type of driving, and I started to wish I'd purchased a vehicle that was higher off the ground and had all-wheel-drive capability. Eventually, I lost cell reception.

As the road finally crested, I saw a brown sign on the right with yellow letters that read, "Elk Pass." I pulled into the trailhead parking and spotted a red Silverado 1500 extended-cab truck with stickers all over the back of national parks and indicating different ultra-races. I knew I was in the right spot and a sense of relief washed over me—I had arrived.

Nobody was with the truck, so I knew they were still out course-marking. I was exhausted and I decided to take a nap while I waited for Paul and Robin to return. I snuggled up with my sleeping bag and tried to get some sleep.

A few hours after midnight, I woke to the sound of a dog barking and a truck door slamming. I looked out the window of my van to see a light mist of rain falling. Through the raindrops, I could see a lanky fellow with a thin brown beard fumbling around in the back of the Chevy truck. He wore a trucker hat backward with a headlamp strapped to his noggin. *This must be Paul*, I thought.

As I got out of the van to greet him, his dog, which looked like some sort of black-and-white husky/Labrador mix, started barking even louder. Evading his dog, I reached out and shook Paul's hand.

"Shut up, Gus! Sit! He's harmless," Paul said, gripping my hand firmly. "So you're Kyle? Thanks for meeting us. How long have you been waiting?"

"A few hours, but I needed the sleep, so it worked out," I replied, trying to escape Paul's grasp.

"Want some food or beer?" He nonchalantly took the bottle cap off his IPA with a Bic lighter.

"No thanks."

"Robin should be along soon. I'm actually surprised I beat her here."

Paul had just gotten done marking seventeen miles of the course. To kill time as we waited, he pulled out a map of the Gifford Pinchot National Forest and laid it across the hood of his truck and illuminated the map with his headlamp. He pointed out our current location and explained our plans for the course-marking process, tracing trails and roads with a highlighter so I could follow along, and he detailed how many miles we would be doing each day, how long it was going to take, and where we would be sleeping each night.

As Paul talked, he polished off a first and then a second IPA. The whole time, he kept looking in the direction Robin was supposed to be coming from. She was marking fifteen miles of trails and should have been back by now.

Finally, out of the blue, Paul shouted, "Marco!" Again, "Marco!" He waited a solid minute and then yelled a third time, "Marco!"

In response, we heard a faint, "Polo!" It was Robin.

In the distance, I saw a light floating in the darkness. Then her dog, Foxy, a dirty-brown Jack Russell terrier, trotted up and greeted us. Finally, I saw the body attached to the headlamp come into full view. "You must be Kyle," she said as she put out her hand to shake mine.

I took her hand and nodded. I wasn't really interested in conversation; I was so out of it from my drive and the time change that I just wanted to go back to bed.

Robin was tall, thin, and outfitted in rain running gear, but I couldn't make out much of her other features due to the darkness around us and her headlamp shining in my eyes. She sat down and proceeded to drink a beer, eat, and feed the dogs, Gus and Foxy, pieces of her sandwich.

Before I crashed on my makeshift bed, they let me know that the next day's plans were not set in stone, which was good, because I had to get up early and go back into town to access the internet for work.

I would soon learn that the people involved in this particular race were a group of ultrarunners who lived in the woods in their cars or tents during the race. They would spend weeks, sometimes even months, setting up for a race. They were a tribe affectionately known as "dirtbag runners."

Unlike many of these runners, I couldn't live completely in the woods. I still had my business to check in on and keep running from afar. But I knew that going into town every day would not be realistic—at least, not if I was going to be a useful volunteer. Plus, it wasn't feasible, as some days we would be over three hours away from civilization and cell reception. We had over a hundred miles of remote trails to mark, and we needed to get it done soon. They didn't have time for a city slicker like me to be going into town every day to check his email and make phone calls. So now that I was out here, I needed to arrange for someone else to answer customer inquiries when I wasn't around.

With that thought, I went to bed. Paul slept in his truck, I in my van, and Robin in her car. I woke well before the others the next morning at around five forty-five. It was cold, the sky was gray, and the clouds hung low, hovering just above the trees. I raced down 131 toward Randle through the potholes and washouts. Finally, I pulled into the parking lot of Mount Adams Cafe at the bottom of the hill and turned on my hotspot internet device; I was in business. I called a friend who had previously agreed to do some work for me while I was gone and gave her a brief crash course on what she needed to do in the event a customer called or emailed. It wasn't complicated, but this was something I should have buttoned up and covered with her before I started my adventure. I left in such a rush I didn't have time. When I was able to have internet access again, I would be able to check in on my business and address any issues or concerns that popped up.

When I returned to the site, Paul and Robin had just gotten up; I was relieved that I hadn't held them up. Paul was sitting in a green camping chair, sipping coffee, and Robin was standing at the back of the Chevy with the tailgate down. A Jetboil was lit in front of her, and she was waiting for it to heat water for her coffee. It seemed like nobody was in a hurry to get the day started. I noticed that under her trucker hat, Robin was wearing her blond hair in pigtails that came down to her shoulders. Her skin was dark and there was a tattoo of a sitting Buddha on her right forearm and an outline of a mountain range on the back of her left calf.

"You get done what you needed to get done?" she asked me.

"Yep, I'm ready to course-mark," I replied happily.

"Want some coffee?"

"Nope, I grabbed some while I was in town."

At that, Robin began explaining the day's plan. It was evident that this was her show, that she knew exactly what she was doing, and that we were just along for the ride. In turn, Robin and Paul could tell right away I had never done anything like this and that I was new to the dirtbag mountain life. Fortunately, they were patient and willing to show me the ropes. I was eager to learn.

"We need to pack our bags for the day first," Robin said. "Do you have a pack?"

I went over to my van and pulled out a small backpack that was big enough for a book and a computer. "Will this work?"

Robin started laughing. "No. I think we have an extra one you can borrow, though." She handed me a big gray backpack that was over five times the size of the one I had pulled out. "When packing, stakes go in first—unless you're a vegetarian, that is." She laughed at her own joke. I put fifteen wooden stakes into my pack, which we would later pound into the ground with a hammer.

"Next are the signs," Robin continued. These were reflective signs with arrows on them, which we would staple to the stakes to point runners in the right direction whenever it was necessary, like when there was a fork in the road or if it was unclear which trail to take. I added twenty of these reflective signs to my pack.

"Now put the dragons in on top."

The course was marked with reflective neon-orange and neon-pink ribbons on wooden clothespins to help runners find their way even in the dark. When the sun went down, the runners could still see a sea of reflective ribbons on trees, rocks, and bushes with their headlamps. To runners on an ultra-marathon course, these "dragons," which we volunteers spent so much time preparing carefully placing along the trail, were their entire life. Without them, they really might die

At this point, the dragons were on a rope called a "dog." The dogs would go around our bodies like a sash so we could easily attach the dragons to the course. We carried five dogs each: four in our pack and one around our body. There were probably a hundred and fifty dragons on each dog. In the near future, I would become very familiar with dragons, as I would be making hundreds of them.

"Finally, you need enough food and water for the trail," Robin said as she was packing her own bag. We made peanut butter and jelly sandwiches and cheese and honey sandwiches and packed several candy bars, along with water. Lots of water—two to three liters per person. When it was all said and done, my pack weighed close to forty pounds.

With our bags packed, the next item on our agenda was figuring out the logistics of course-marking: shuttling our cars around and deciding what needed to be marked, who was going to mark what, who was going to end up where, how we were going to get back, and where we were going to park the three vehicles.

First, we shuttled Robin's car to where we were all going to meet: the Spencer Butte aid station. Then we dropped Robin off with the dogs at the Road 9327 aid station. She was going to mark from there to Spencer Butte. Paul and I drove on to the Lewis River. We were going to mark from there to Spencer Butte, so that all of us ended up at the same place when we were done marking.

Evidently, before I showed up, there had been another volunteer who lived nearby, but he'd left because Paul and Robin were fighting too much about logistics. I didn't feel like I had the option to just leave because I was so far from home and had invested a lot of money and energy in this adventure. Anyhow, I didn't really have anywhere else to go. Also, after my childhood, being around people who were constantly fighting was something I was used to.

Once Paul and I reached the Lewis River, we strapped on our packs and set off to mark. It was slow going at first because I had no idea what I was doing. Paul had to tell me where to clip the dragons on the trees and where to staple a sign or hammer in a stake. I watched him in his orange-and-blue-striped tank top place a dragon seemingly at random or take one of mine down, trying to understand the method.

Making things more difficult was the fact that we were traversing the course backward. That is, we were marking in the opposite direction from the way the runners would be going. Therefore, every time we put up an arrow, we had to turn around and be sure it was facing the right direction. I was surprised at how many times we had to adjust the arrows.

Paul described himself as a rock-climbing bum, and he told me how he had met Robin a few years back in Washington State where she was from originally. She was out there volunteering for other races and he happened to be hiking the same trail at the time. They got to talking and learned they both lived in South Lake Tahoe just a few blocks from each other. Paul was cool, funny, and easygoing, the kind of guy who was nice to everyone unless someone crossed him—and even after that, he might still give them the benefit of the doubt.

As we were heading up the trail, Paul told me he was originally from Colorado and had family there. He said he hadn't been back in years and had just been traveling and rock climbing as much as he could and he loved living near Lake Tahoe. I assumed there was more to his story he wasn't sharing—I could relate, and I respected his boundaries. It did make me feel good to know others have things going on in their life they're trying to work out similar to me. I really enjoyed listening to Paul as we fast-tracked down the trail marking as we went. We discovered our mutual interests in skateboarding and motorcycles and bonded over that. It was nice to talk and hear about other interests and outlets outside of trail running.

We saw very few people on the trail and even got lost a few times. After the first time, I realized that this was the norm; getting lost was just part of course-marking. Luckily, we were equipped with a high-powered GPS with the trail marked on it, so we could navigate our way back. Of course, that was only if the GPS was accurate and fully charged. Sometimes, it was neither.

Whenever we did run into other people on the trails, we had to explain ourselves and what we were doing for several reasons: first, as a couple of guys running or walking down the trail with a bunch of neon ribbons wrapped around our bodies and large packs strapped to our backs, we definitely looked odd; second, we needed to let people know that the markers were for an actual purpose so they wouldn't take them down; third, we had to let people know we weren't crazy or stoned; fourth, people were just curious; and fifth, some of these people hadn't seen another human on the trail for quite some time, and it was simply nice to talk to them and learn why they were also out there and where they were from.

I was surprised by how many people would want to sabotage someone's race by taking down the course markings we were putting up. It was mostly people who thought we were denigrating the serenity of the forest or teenagers pulling a prank. I wasn't really surprised by the latter group though, because I probably would have done the same thing when I was a teenager if I had seen the markings. Of course, it would have been a better prank if they turned the arrow signs to point in a different direction and then placed the dragons going in that direction instead, leading runners down a different path, as opposed to just taking the markings down. That would really have gotten a lot of runners lost. Truly, these kids were prank amateurs.

I spent the next few sunny days marking with Paul, and then at night, we met Robin back at camp. We were all friends having a good time. Whoever returned to the campsite first had to make dinner and have it ready for the others when they arrived. It made the whole process into a challenge, a race, and a goal to shoot for. No matter when we arrived though, seeing the cars at the end of the day gave us an amazing feeling.

My first few outings marking the course with Paul were quite the experience. I saw snow-capped Mount Adams and the blown-off summit of Mount Saint Helens. The trails were a lot narrower and very technical with an abundance of roots, rocks and other obstacles, making them much more dangerous than the ones I was used to in Ohio, and the elevation was nothing like what I had experienced before. There were times when I looked down into the valley hundreds of yards below and the only thing that prevented me from going over the edge was my own balance.

Not only did I get to see great landscapes and amazing scenery, but we also met a few interesting people. On our second day of marking, Paul and I entered a clearing and saw a white late-sixties VW bus with the paint chipping off the side. As we walked over to investigate, we found a man in his mid-forties with thinning black hair and a clean shave standing in front of a deer hide about the size of a bedsheet stretched between the trees.

Paul took the lead. "Hey! Whatcha doing?"

"Oh, man! Hey, guys, welcome! My name's Dan." Dan appeared

to be very excited to see us. "I'm getting this hide ready. I'll be wearing it for the ceremony."

"What ceremony?" Paul asked.

Dan pointed up the hill in the direction opposite where we'd come from, where there was no path. "Vision quest. Up there. We built a sweat lodge. I'll be leading the quest. That's what this hide is for."

At the time, out in the woods, this seemed like a reasonable explanation. Afterward, not so much. Still, Dan seemed like the happiest guy in the world as he prepared his deer hide.

The next day, as night was approaching, I was waiting for Paul to meet me back at the truck when a green Ford Ranger pickup pulled up beside me. Inside was a couple in their early thirties, and they were ready to party.

A young woman with a black ponytail and a white midriff-baring tank top exited the truck and asked me if I had a pump she could borrow to inflate their air mattress. They would be camping there for the night. I grabbed our pump from the truck and handed it to her.

"What's your name?" she asked.

"Kyle. You?"

"I'm Tetris Superstar. Nice to meet you," she replied, and did some kind of odd curtsy. "We have some mushrooms. Would you like some?"

I laughed and declined her offer. That was the thing about being out in the middle of nowhere: anyone could be whoever they wanted to be, and nobody questioned it.

Later that evening, we went by Tetris Superstar's camp, and we could hear the music blaring from a distance. There were a few more cars at their site now, and they had set up a disco light, which was illuminating the forest canopy, spinning and changing colors. It looked amazing. I suppose Tetris and her beau were on their own kind of vision quest. I should have told them to meet up with Dan.

After several days of course-marking, we needed to go back into town to get supplies and prepare to meet up with some other volunteers who'd be helping mark the rest of the course. The mere mention of going back into town was music to my ears; I would be able to check in on work and clean myself up a bit. I hadn't showered in almost a week, and I knew it was even longer for Robin and Paul. I couldn't remember the last time I had gone that long without a shower, but I didn't really mind because we were all in the same boat. We decided to stay at a local campground in Randle—Cascade Peaks—so we could shower, have a fire and a few beers, and wait for the others to meet us the next day.

The plan was for me to go into town earlier alone so I could reserve the campsite and pick up some packages that had been sent to race HQ. While I was in town, Robin and Paul finished marking a section of the route.

In town, I secured the campsite, picked up the packages, took care of my business, and took a shower. Robin and Paul completed course-marking early enough to join me for a late lunch.

I met them at our favorite spot, Mt. Adams Cafe. I arrived first, and then Paul joined me. He slid into the booth across from me, facing the café's entrance. Paul had changed into a red-and-black flannel shirt with gray stripes throughout. Robin appeared later, wearing her usual trucker hat with her long blond hair in two braids on either side falling past her shoulders.

In that moment, I felt happy as we ate lunch and talked about the past few days on the trails and what was coming up. This was exactly what I had come out here for: to spend time on the trails and meet new friends. I didn't know where this journey would take me—if all I was going to get out of it was a few new friends, or if it was the start of a whole new "dirtbag runner" lifestyle, but I tried not to worry about that. For now, I was content.

CHAPTER 8

The Sheriff

By the time Paul, Robin, and I had returned to HQ the following morning, other volunteers had shown up, and we were all busy organizing food and supplies. This time tomorrow, we would be marking the blast zone of Mount Saint Helens and beyond.

After loading the supplies in everyone's vehicles, it was time to head to the campsite where we'd continue the course marking. I rode out there with another volunteer, Robby. With long, black hair and a long beard twisted at the end with rubber bands, Robby looked like a younger version of Rob Zombie. He was usually wearing a Punisher-type shirt with a skull on it and had faded stick-and-poke tattoos of demons and scary clown faces up his arms. He looked more like a mixed martial artist fighter than a trail runner, towering well over six feet tall. We followed behind Paul, who was riding with Robin. I left my van behind because it wasn't going to fare well on the remote roads and I would be sleeping in just my Walmart tent.

We traveled by way of unmarked ranger roads, which made the whole voyage a lot longer. Right before dusk, we arrived at a dead-end road that led directly into the blast zone of Mount Saint Helens. Waiting for us at a makeshift campsite were two other runners/volunteers, Justin and Patrick. They were a little older, both in their late forties or early fifties, and were standing by a fire drinking beer when we pulled up. It seemed they had been waiting for some time by the excitement of their voices and how much they were talking even before I stepped foot out of Robby's car.

That night, we made hundreds of dragons around the fire and figured out who would be course-marking the next day. It became clear that the only two people who were able to actually course-mark were Robin and myself. Justin and Patrick were running the race, and they didn't want to log that many miles beforehand. Robby was injured and couldn't really mark; plus, we needed him to shuttle us around. The plan was for Robin and me to start marking right from the blast zone where we were camped. Robby would meet us at our end point with supplies and our tents so we could continue to course-mark the next day. Paul, Justin, and Patrick would drive around and set up signs on the road and trailheads.

Before we left the next morning, I went toward the dead-end road just beyond our campsite and looked into the clearing ahead. Before me was Mount Saint Helens and the aftermath of its volcanic eruption. Robin and I were set to venture into this blast zone with our packs stuffed full of course-marking gear. The scenery was like nothing I'd ever seen. At first, we were in a regular forest surrounded by green trees and foliage. Then before I knew it, we were exposed without shade and with the sun beating down on us, surrounded by gray rocks and ash from the 1980 volcanic eruption.

Twenty or so miles later, we finished the day's marking and ended at the Johnston Ridge Observatory in the heart of the blast zone. We ran down the paved path to the parking lot, where Robby was waiting for us with a veggie burger for me, a hamburger for Robin, and our sleeping gear. By this time it had started raining, my knees hurt, and I was exhausted and happy to just be sitting.

The temperature was dropping quickly and it would be getting dark soon, so we piled into Robby's car and took off to find a place to camp. Because of the weather and how dark it was, we pulled into the first parking lot we saw. The entrance had a sign that read, "No camping, no fires, no alcohol, and no firearms." Naturally this was the ideal place for us to stay for the night. We set up our tents behind Robby's car, as if a ranger couldn't see them there. We all cracked open some beers, I lit a fire using the wooden stakes from marking, and we all gathered around the fire in our canvas camping chairs.

"If only somebody had a gun, we would be in violation of all the rules here," I said jokingly.

Without missing a beat, Robby ran his fingers over his beard as if he were thinking, set down his beer, got out of his green camping chair, and headed toward his driver-side door. When he reappeared, he was holding a black nine-millimeter pistol.

Maybe it's normal for people out here in the middle of nowhere to carry a gun, I thought. Aloud, I said, "We are so fucked if a ranger pulls in here. We're breaking *all* the rules." Which was thrilling and scary at the same time.

"What the hell do you have that for?" Robin asked.

"Ya never know. I have a concealed-carry permit," Robby explained.

"Let's put that away," I said. Triple B used to own guns that he never locked up properly: he kept a pistol in his nightstand, with bullets, and also had a few rifles in his closet. The older I got, the more I felt it was a miracle that none of us kids ever messed around with them and hurt ourselves—or that Triple B never pulled one out in anger. In any case, as an adult, I wasn't really a fan of guns and got nervous when they were around.

We were, essentially, in the middle of nowhere and I didn't know Robby that well, so I thought it would be best if guns were not part of that evening's activities. Robby put the gun back where he'd gotten it and we continued to drink and talk.

Luckily, a ranger didn't show up that night, and we all went to sleep in our separate tents. In the morning, I woke up in a drenched sleeping bag, dragged myself out of my waterlogged tent. My Walmart tent didn't provide me much protection from the elements. As I zipped open my tent I was greeted by the sight of more rain and gray clouds. Doing another long trek on the trails didn't seem appealing to me. We cleaned up the ashes from our fire and made our way to the start of the next course-marking section, a daunting distance of nineteen miles that stretched from Coldwater Lake to Norway Pass.

The course-marking started with a brutal six-mile narrow ascent into the Wenatchee National Forest. We hiked up snow-covered trails, passed mountain goats, and gradually climbed to the summit of Mount Margaret. Although I was exhausted, I was energized by the scenery. Once we got high enough, I was able to look down and see the crystal-blue water of Spirit Lake near the base of Mount Saint Helens. I could see thousands of pyrolyzed trees floating on the surface of the lake from the volcanic eruption. It was a sight to see. I kept telling myself how lucky I was to be able to experience all this.

As Robin and I ended our journey down into Norway Pass, we saw Robby's car in the trailhead parking lot and started screaming at the top of our lungs and running down the hill toward it. Both of us were excited to be done and to get some real food in our bellies.

As soon as we got to the parking lot, I lay down on the ground with a smile on my face, exhausted. For the most part, the course-marking was now done. We made our way back to Randle to meet up with the rest of the volunteers at the race headquarters.

Before we left the mountain, I decided to go to a hotel and shower. It was nice to have a roof over my head, and I was able to take a shower and do my laundry. Plus, internet access meant I could do some work. I laid out my tent in the field in front of the hotel and let it dry out. Although I was around a TV for the first time in over a week, I had no desire to watch it. I didn't care what was going on in the world, and I didn't want to know.

I packed up, got in my van, and drove back toward race HQ with a pit in my stomach. For some reason, I was feeling hesitant and scared. I kept thinking to myself, *What are you doing, Kyle? This is crazy. You should just leave. It's time to go back to reality, you've had your adventure.* I knew that's what my friends from back home would have told me. But I didn't leave. Something told me that no matter where the adventure led me, it was where I was supposed to be. I thought back to my old friends Carl and Tommy sitting around at the Winking Lizard Tavern, drinking and watching the Cleveland Browns lose another game. Maybe it was good that I wasn't feeling comfortable here. Maybe that was the point.

I pulled into the HQ parking lot and saw that there were even more volunteers now. "What do you need me to do?" I asked Paul, who was organizing food and supplies for aid stations.

Paul looked up at me and smiled. "Good to have you back. We're just organizing supplies for the different aid stations. Why don't you help Debbie and see what she needs?"

I smiled back at him. I don't know why I considered leaving—this was where I belonged at this moment. Immediately, I felt like I was part of the tribe—not just the tribe but the inner circle. I walked over to Debbie in the shed, which was basically where the school stored its batting cages and sports supplies. The nets for the cages were all moved to the back of the shed to make room for the food and supplies designated for each aid station. Debbie was the race director in charge of organizing the entire race. She also had to make sure all the aid stations had the supplies they needed to keep the runners fed and warm. There were thirteen separate piles—one for each aid station—and a sign on the wall indicating which station each pile was for. When the aid station captains came to pick up their supplies, we would have it all ready to go for them, thanks to a detailed checklist.

Aid stations at ultramarathons are like buffets. There are choices of fruits: bananas, watermelon, oranges, grapes, and more. Runners can also get pretty much any sugary snack they desire: M&M's, gummy bears, cookies, and granola bars. It's all there. There's also hot food, such as pancakes, tacos, grilled cheese, hamburgers, and soup. Fluids are abundant, too, and racers can get endless amounts of water, electrolyte-heavy sports drinks, running gels, all kinds of soda, coffee, and tea. There are heaters, coolers, ice, tents, and sleeping pads, all so the runners can stay full, hydrated, and well rested to complete the grueling race.

Transporting all of these supplies, plus the gas, butane, and generators to run the aid station properly, can be a major challenge. The race would be going through some very remote parts of the Cascades, and we would need an all-wheel-drive vehicle to get to some of the destinations. To save on supplies, once an early aid station closes down, the volunteers pack it all up and move the supplies to a later aid station location.

I worked alongside other volunteers whom I would be spending the next several months with: Brian, Pam, Debbie, and Robby, who had been shuttling us around earlier. Brian was from Oregon, and he was short with blond hair and a trimmed blond beard. Debbie, who we affectionately called "Auntie" because she seemed like a relative to us all based on how she was looking out for us, had dark hair and was from Washington State and was essentially running the show. Pam was a military vet with short black hair; we called her "Sarge."

Getting a trail name is a kind of rite of passage in this world. Mine was "Sheriff," on account of my being a lawyer. Robin was "Jeopardy" because people would always ask her questions as if she had all the answers. Paul was "Hermit" because he liked to be alone. Robby was "Gunner" for obvious reasons. Once I received my trail name, it felt like I was truly part of the tribe.

Everyone who had the honor of a trail name also had to wear a trucker hat at all times—every single one of us wore one. We were all from different parts of the country with different personalities, but the trail brought us together.

We were also bound together by how dirty we were. We went days without showering, sometimes even weeks. We did have the option of a solar shower, but it sounds a lot warmer than it actually is. Basically, it's a plastic bag filled with water and left out in the sun to get warm. Once someone is ready to shower, they just prop the bag up on a hook, get underneath it, and clean as much dirt and odor off of them as they can. It can be difficult to prop the bag up because of its weight, and sometimes, they might have to sit down to shower because the bag hangs so low. A solar shower won't get someone as clean as a regular shower, but when someone smells terrible and they haven't showered for days on end, it's amazing how clean they can feel after that.

I spent most of my down time getting to know Robby and Brian.

Robby in particular was someone I had a hard time imagining being friends with back in Cleveland—or anywhere else, for that matter. He was unlike just about anyone I'd ever met: A vegetarian who drove a blue Jeep Wrangler decked out in snake and skull stickers. I wouldn't have taken him for a seasoned ultrarunner, but looks can be deceiving—I quickly learned that he had completed many 100-plus-mile races. His wife and daughter lived back home in Yakima, Washington, where Robby lived and worked construction. However, not all looks are deceiving. Robby was in fact, an amateur MMA fighter and was eager to show us videos on his phone—though in the one we all watched together, he got beat up pretty quickly. He was a bit of a survivalist and knew better than me how to camp, hunt, build fires. Though he and the others welcomed me into the flock pretty readily, I always wondered how I must have seemed to someone like Robby. I had something many of them couldn't imagine—a desk job of sorts. I imagine I must have seemed like a real outsider, maybe someone just experimenting with the lifestyle they seemed to embody.

Brian said he was a triathlete trainer back home, though he didn't seem to be doing much work while he was out here with us. More of a mountain biker than a trail runner, he wanted to get more of a feel for running the trails. I got the sense that he, like me, was also trying to find his way in life and was looking for an adventure. He drove a red Honda Element with an extendable tent on the roof—he was definitely the type to have all the latest gadgets. I felt woefully unprepared, looking at his new solar lights, the most advanced GPS watch, the best action camera. When I hurt my knee, he lent me a device that gave electric pulses to stimulate the muscle to health. He was also an amateur photographer always taking pictures of the landscape and the stars. He was a nice guy, and we bonded almost immediately.

Together, Brian, Robby, and I would scrabble up mountains or camp when we got the chance, trying to see the highest elevation we could get to before we had problems breathing, or before it wasn't safe anymore, or before we ran out of water. They, like me, were out here for the long haul, volunteering for the entire period, and so we got to know each other well. And I learned more from them during that time than I could have learned from any camping or survivalist course.

I still remember camping one night in the middle of the Cascade Mountains when a different volunteer, a woman named Pamela, made us burritos. Not a camping version of burritos but a delicious meal complete with fixings packed into a burrito shell and baked over a fire. For someone like me who'd mostly bought basic camping food from REI and had been prepared for hot dogs and s'mores at most, this was mind-blowing.

Pamela, along with pretty much everyone else I encountered, seemed so much more comfortable and adept to the situation and environment. But they welcomed me into their tribe nonetheless, and every day I fell a little more in love with life out in the mountains. In Ohio or Michigan, you camped at KOAs where campers were on top of each other, dozens of tents and RVs squeezed in together.

But out here? Your neighbors were wild animals—bears, cougars, mountain goats, coyotes. There was a little fear in it, a little danger. And I liked that part, too.

The day before the race began, all of the runners met in the school for a pre-race meeting. Debbie explained aid stations and how the race would go. Paul, Robin, and I went over the course in mile-by-mile detail, explaining where the aid stations were, what the terrain was like, and where they might be able to find water if they ran out. This meeting was also where all of our course-marking became particularly valuable. We were able to give details on the exact terrain from just days before when we ran and marked the course. I even contacted the local paper, and they came to report on the race.

The next day, the runners started their journey at Marble Mountain, which is also the starting point for climbing Mount Saint Helens in the winter. Before the runners started, we equipped each of them with a GPS tracker.

Most runners had "crew," a group of people that would drive to each aid station, tend to their runner's specific needs, and bring specialty items that were not at the aid stations. Not every runner had a crew though, and in these cases, the runners were allowed to drop bags, packed with additional essential supplies, at certain aid stations in advance. When a runner arrived at an aid station, their drop bag would already be there, waiting. These bags might include a change of shoes or clothes, extra batteries for their headlamp, or aspirin. Then there were pacers. These were runners who would join someone experiencing a tough or low point and keep them company during their race.

Once the runners took off, there wasn't much to do except hang around at home base and wait to see if any aid stations needed more supplies. We had a good communication apparatus: at headquarters, we all had two-way radios, which had about a mile or so of coverage. There were also ham radio operators at HQ and at each aid station, so we could keep in touch.

At one point, we received word that the Twin Sisters aid station needed more water and food. Debbie was going to drive Paul's truck up, hauling the supplies, and I decided to keep her company. Debbie had been given her trail name "Auntie" for a good reason, and it wasn't just because she had three nieces of her own and was always looking out for us. She made sure everyone had what they needed and would dole out motherly advice, all while directing the race. She was also one of my closest friends on my adventure. After knowing her for a few days, I already felt like I could tell her anything.

It was a long drive up the mountain to Twin Sisters and as we drove, we passed truckloads of people driving back down the mountain who had been up there picking berries to sell in town. I decided to take full advantage of Debbie's motherly advice. We talked about our lives and what was going on back home with each of us. I brought up my life in Ohio and how I struggled in school, and had problems with the law, but eventually got on, somewhat, the right track. I spoke of how I was out here trying to find a version of myself that made me happy. I really didn't get into the details of my relationship with Triple B. I wasn't ready to share that yet, with Debbie, or anyone else. Debbie told me about how she had a husband back home, and it was hard to be away for weeks at a time.

It felt really good to talk with someone about my struggles, though. It's interesting, looking back now, how I ran into people in my life that were like North Stars, pointing me in the right direction. I had that with Mr. Bishop, Mr. Brady, Gary, and now Debbie. Debbie knew racing and trail running almost better than anyone else. She told me how, as I may be learning, living and traveling constantly isn't the most glamorous lifestyle. She continued, and told me how it's hard to put down roots and grow real lasting relationships on the road. I soaked in what she was saying as we drove down the bumpy road. It was nice to get someone's perspective who was actually living the lifestyle that I, and others on social media, fantasized about. It's like a lot of things in life, not everything is as it seems. She told me that she was very happy I'd made the long trip out here and that I had been a big help.

Debbie looked over at me as she was driving and pointed out the window. I could see the picturesque Mount Adams through the driver-side window beyond her trucker hat – it looked like a painting. "This is what it's all about," Debbie said with a smile. She usually wore a smile.

We occasionally saw runners who had quit or heard stories about runners who had gotten lost and gone off the trail but eventually found their way back on. Then we received word that the first runner was a few miles from the finish line. To finish in such a short amount of time meant they didn't rest much at all. It was a big event to see the first-place finisher, and we all cheered. Runners started trickling in after that until the DFL—Dead Fucking Last—runner came in. That seemed to be an even bigger event than the winner, because they needed to beat the final cutoff time, which built up a lot of drama, and all the other finishers were there to see them finish. This last runner made it by only a few minutes, adding to our excitement.

After each racer finished, they got to sit down on a chair, and a personalized pizza was prepared for them from a portable stove. One of the first questions they were asked upon crossing the finish line was, "What do you want on your pizza?" It was best when we knew what kind of pie they wanted before they even finished. When they were a mile or so out, we would get their order, so that their fresh pizza was ready and waiting for them.

The awards ceremony was the next day. Debbie handed out awards to the top finishers, and they also made up silly, fun awards. There were awards for best hallucination, an award for helping out another runner in a jam, the DFL award, and so on. The volunteers also got special recognition, including course-marking awards in the form of a dragon: a handmade clothespin had been cut and shaped into an actual dragon.

We spent that night drinking and celebrating with the runners. The next day, we cleaned up. We had to be out of HQ by the end of the day. Even with seven people working, it took most of the day to clean and load up the trailer. Soon, everyone was leaving and saying their goodbyes. It was over.

There was another race out by Lake Tahoe, California in two weeks that Debbie was organizing, and I wanted to be a part of it. Plus, because Paul and Robin both lived in South Lake Tahoe, it would make course marking easier because we could work out of one of their homes until race day. My journey in the trail running world, it seemed, wasn't yet ready to end.

CHAPTER 9

Rescue Mission

After the race in Washington was over and all the runners had gone home, I typed "Cleveland, Ohio" into my GPS. I had been gone a little over a month at this point, and I needed to check on my apartment and pick up the mail that had been piling up. Besides, I didn't really have anywhere else to go, and I needed to recuperate for Tahoe. Hell, at this point, I was fantasizing about sleeping in my own bed.

I told Robby, Brian, Paul, and Robin I was just driving around the Pacific Northwest, maybe going as far as Colorado to do some exploring. I didn't want to look like a crazy person going all the way back to Ohio when I was, possibly, going to be volunteering out at the race in Tahoe.

As I approached the Ohio state line and saw signs that read "Cleveland—101 Miles," I got a weird feeling. This feeling only intensified as I got closer to Ohio and farther away from the mountains. It was a feeling of dread over what was waiting for me there: my old self. Not that I was a new person. I was still me, unable to confront my past or the mistakes I had made or was making. Apparently, Ohio now represented a lot of the mistakes, shame, and trauma I carried within me. It had been so nice to be around different people with different mindsets and different lifestyles. I was trying to block all that out of my mind and focus on the possibilities of my future. Ohio was a very different world from the one I had just left behind, and I didn't want to face it. I took a deep breath and told myself I'd only be there for a week or so. On the bright side, being back in Ohio did give me some peace of mind, because I was able to focus on work for a bit and be able to see Chris, PJ, and Baby. Plus, it was nice knowing that my apartment hadn't gone up in flames and I hadn't been robbed.

After spending a little over a week in Ohio focusing on work and meeting up with my friends for a run or two, I was able and ready to take another extended trip. I left once again, this time making the cross-country drive to Lake Tahoe. I was getting so used to logging so many miles and sleeping in the van, it didn't bother me too much anymore. Before arriving, I stopped at REI in Reno and finally purchased some real camping gear and supplies—I was turning into a real dirtbag outdoorsman.

I arrived in Tahoe over Labor Day weekend, several days before Debbie had asked everyone to be there. As I drove into Lake Tahoe, I passed Squaw Valley, where the legendary Western States hundred-miler starts. I got a chill just being in the area. The Western States 100 is the premier event in ultrarunning. It's like the Super Bowl or the Daytona 500 for ultrarunners. I decided to spend these extra few days exploring the area and trails. The closest campsite I could find with vacancy was on the western side of Lake Tahoe—the William Kent Campground. The campground there wasn't equipped with showers, but it did have potable water, a campfire ring in each campsite, and a place to park my van and relax. The campsite was a quick walk from the lake, and I took advantage of this fact by jumping in as soon as I arrived.

My early camping experiences had all been on the east side of the country. Before Washington, I had never camped in the middle of nowhere—it was always at a designated campsite. Because these campsites were near civilization, the closest I'd ever gotten to "real" wildlife was the occasional deer, raccoon, or squirrel. I'd been more likely to encounter a drunken neighbor who stumbled over from their campsite than a bear.

Camping in the western portion of the US at designated spots was a learning experience for me. Every designated campsite in the West had big metal containers with locks on the outside that were used as bear food storage bins. Not bins to store food for bears, but rather to store food so that bears wouldn't eat it. I had to put all food in these bins, even things like gum. If it had a smell, it had to go in there. I couldn't even leave it in my van, because bears could still smell it and were able to break into vehicles. I assume some campsites in the East probably had the same bear boxes—but not the campsites I frequented.

It was nice to be back in nature and in a new place I had yet to explore. Tahoe is obviously quite different from Washington and I went for a run on the Tahoe Rim Trail to check out the landscape when I first arrived. After the remote Cascade Range of Washington, where I might not run into anyone on the trails at all, Tahoe seemed strange, and I was initially unimpressed. I couldn't seem to escape the crowds of tourists enjoying the holiday weekend as I sped up the trail, constantly running into hikers and mountain bikers. However, I would soon learn that I was only scratching the surface of what Tahoe had to offer and that it had its own unique features, which I would soon fall in love with.

On my second day there, I met up with Brian, who would be volunteering again with me. It was nice to see another person from that race and to have someone else to explore the area with. Brian had never been to Tahoe before either, so he was just as eager as I was to see what it had to offer and was better at locating cool trails and areas to explore. I was quickly reminded how comfortable Brian was with being outdoors and in nature, especially by contrast; he sometimes referred to me as "city boy." We went swimming and running on the trails and gambling at the casino together. We were basically just killing time. Debbie informed me on my drive to Tahoe that volunteers would be meeting up at Robin's house because she lived out there and to wait until I hear from her for instructions.

Robin finally reached out to us and told us we could come over early to stay at her place because she had extra space. However, her mother and her mother's husband were also there. Brian and I felt weird about showing up and interrupting family time. Brian and I decided not to go over that night, and we camped out nearby her house in our vehicles.

We decided to head over to Robin's house the next day. I figured that they had gotten their family time in by now. Even though Robin's mom and stepfather were still there, we were assured it was okay to intrude. The extra room with bunk beds was for Brian and me.

Her house was located west of Lake Valley on the south rim of Lake Tahoe and was situated in such a way that a set of rickety stairs on the side of the house led up to a back deck. Brian and I arrived late afternoon with the sun still shining. Paul, who lived close by, was already there and on the porch with an older gentleman with white hair and glasses. I surmised this was Robin's stepfather, Don. He was standing in front of the grill in Hawaiian shorts and a white polo shirt with a spatula in his hand and flipping burgers. After a few pleasantries, we proceeded through the sliding glass door inside, where Robin was with her mom, Sophie.

"Thanks for inviting us over," I said with a smile. "Sorry about not coming over yesterday. We just didn't feel right about it."

"Not a problem. You're here now," Robin said cheerfully.

That night, we all ate what Don had grilled for dinner, and enjoyed each other's company. The next morning, we dragged ourselves out of bed and gulped down coffee. Soon, Debbie and other volunteers would be showing up, and we would be starting preparations in earnest. We would have to make new direction signs and a whole lot of dragons. Working at Robin's house was a much more convenient work setup than we had out in the woods; here, we had an actual home to work out of with the added benefits of bathrooms, showers, a kitchen, and civilization if we needed anything.

The next day, we started course-marking the trails of Tahoe. I was marking with Robin, while Paul led another team. As we course marked, Debbie prepared the food to head out to the aid stations. Once we got on the trails and away from Tahoe City and the tourists, my mind quickly changed about not being impressed with Tahoe. It was warm enough that I was able to jump into half a dozen lakes, and I got the chance to run along the Rubicon Trail and the Barrett jeep trails. As in Washington, we would camp wherever we ended up.

One day, our course-marking had us ending up at Loon Lake, west of Tahoe. We met up with Paul and his group of course-marking volunteers. It was still daylight when we all finished, and we were able to set up the tents that a volunteer had shuttled there earlier, along with additional supplies. It was the perfect end to a long day and a great location, except for one fact: the yellow jackets. They were swarming everywhere. Sure, we had noticed them on the trail as we went along, but we hadn't considered them to be much of a nuisance. Once we were at the campsite, however, it was as if we were standing in the middle of their nest. We couldn't do anything without being targeted by these weaponized insects. Forget about opening any food or drinks; they would be on it before anyone's mouth could get near it.

Suddenly, Robin screamed, "*Damn it!* I just got stung."

"Fuck, me too!" shouted Paul.

Not two minutes later, Brian and I were also victims of their stingers.

We had to be concerned about the yellow jackets because there would be an aid station at Loon Lake during the race, and if the yellow jackets were going to be this bad, we needed to address it. We ended up getting dozens of yellow jacket traps to hang at each aid station, which seemed to minimize their fury. Fortunately, yellow jackets go away once it's dark out, and they stay away from the fire in general. Despite all of our best efforts, there would be reports of at least a dozen runners, volunteers, and crew members who got stung during the race.

Camping out in the middle of nowhere was one of my favorite things after course-marking for twenty or thirty miles a day. At night, I could clearly see billions of stars in the sky. When we didn't have cell reception, we were able to enjoy each other's company, talk, and drink. It made me feel like I didn't have a care in the world. We'd prepare food by the fire, play cards, and even set up a slackline at times for fun. We turned course-marking into a game, pitting Robin's team against Paul's team to see who could get done first. This made it more exciting because the losing team would have to buy dinner and drinks. It usually wasn't fair, though, because both Robin and I were so competitive. We would take it a bit too seriously and practically sprint along the course, yelling at other volunteers to hurry up.

Some days, the trails in Tahoe were saturated with mountain bikers, and at one point, we even got caught in the middle of a mountain bike race. We had to step aside while dozens of bikes raced past us. It got so annoying that at one point, Robin, who was an avid mountain biker, mumbled under her breath, "Fucking bikers." One biker heard this and stopped in her tracks and looked as if she wanted to punch us in the face. Luckily, we were heading the other way. We started running as fast as we could, laughing along the way. During all these moments on the trail I never wished or yearned to be somewhere else.

We ended up finishing course-marking early, which gave us some time to relax a bit before the race. Plus, we needed to help Debbie do a little more aid-station prep, since Tahoe had more participants than the Washington race. On the bright side, it was a bit easier, because we had more volunteers than we'd had in Washington. By this point we left Robin's house and we were all strictly hanging out at headquarters—a ski resort on the west side of Lake Tahoe. We had a trailer with supplies and a few canopy tents set up. As in Washington, volunteers picked up their aid station supplies from us and headed out. Resupplying aid stations would be easier and a bit less stressful, because they were all easily accessible, unlike in Washington, and most aid stations had cell reception so they could just call in when they were short on supplies.

I spent a lot of my time before the race going from aid station to aid station, helping volunteers set up their tents or canopies or bringing supplies. It was an amazing way to see Tahoe. Not only was I able to run around the whole area on foot, I was able to drive around several times to see the landscape.

One of the worst parts about volunteering was going to an aid station after it had closed down and making sure everything had been cleaned up properly. Aid station captains were supposed to ensure that the stations were cleaned up, which included taking all garbage to the proper receptacles. Most aid stations didn't have dumpsters. Therefore trash would have to be taken away in a volunteer's car, sometimes for quite a distance, to throw it out. Some aid stations left their garbage because it "wouldn't fit in their car." This seemed to be an issue with many aid stations, so I was often responsible for picking up the garbage that any aid stations left behind. Once I picked up my first such bag, I understood why it "wouldn't fit in their car": the smelly, sometimes leaking bags were an assault on the senses.

One day I met a young couple that was in charge of an aid station. They were from Southern California but had clearly been part of the larger ultra community for a while and knew many of the runners and hikers who were coming in and out. And yet they had never run an aid station before, so it was my responsibility to show them what to do and how it worked. It was a surreal experience for me, sharing knowledge that I had just learned in the last few months, as if I were some sort of expert. But to them, I was. So, I showed them the best way to set up the tent and the food/water, the grill, and when to expect the first runners. I showed them what to do in the event that someone was sick and needed medical care.

How on earth did I get here? I thought. *Is this really who I am now?* I felt a flicker of worry—everything that happened at that aid station would be my responsibility. Of course everything ran smoothly. And for a moment, that young couple made me feel as if I were actually who I wanted to be at that moment—another van dweller out west, living my fantasy.

It was the first night after the start of the race and the sun would soon be going down, and I was almost ten thousand feet above sea level on a single-track trail near South Lake Tahoe running as fast as my legs would carry me. With every stride, my breath became increasingly labored. Glancing down through the tall pine trees as I climbed higher and higher above the Heavenly Ski Resort parking lot, I could see the eastern shore of Lake Tahoe glistening in the sun and the casinos and hotels in the basin of Stateline, Nevada. I wasn't dressed properly for the weather that was coming, wearing only my blue running shirt and black running shorts. Although it was close to seventy degrees at the moment, I knew the temperature could quickly drop to below freezing once the sun faded behind mountains. I hadn't thought I'd be out on the mountain this long, but there I was, still going, because Tim was lost, and somehow it had become my responsibility to find him.

Mile four turned into mile five, which turned into mile six, and so on, as I ascended the hill. The farther I ran, the more frustrated I became. *How could he get lost? The course is well marked, and it's still daylight. Where the fuck are you, Tim?*

A few hours earlier, we had received word from Paul, who was tracking Tim, along with every other runner participating in the ultramarathon race, that Tim was off course. Way off course. All the runners were equipped with a spot tracker, which they kept attached to their running packs at all times so that Paul at race headquarters could track them via satellite. If runners were in trouble, they were able to call for help with the spot tracker by pressing a distress signal button. That, in turn, would let race HQ know, and hopefully, someone would be able to locate and rescue them.

"The spot tracker has Tim, bib number forty-seven, off course.

He's pressed the emergency distress button three times to signal for help," Paul had said, his voice echoing through the radio.

I could hear the distress in his voice, and I imagined his thumb turning white from all the blood rushing out of it as he pressed down hard on the two-way radio button to communicate with Debbie, on the other end.

Debbie and I were standing next to each other outside of a canopy tent at Tunnel Creek aid station, where the runners could refuel and get some rest, on the eastern side of Lake Tahoe.

"*What?*" she said, her voice tinged with concern. "What do you mean?" Runners were only supposed to signal for help in a dire emergency. If the emergency button was pressed, we had to consider it a life-and-death situation.

"We have a runner who is off course, lost, and needs help. His last check-in was at the Heavenly aid station a few hours ago," Paul said again, this time more urgently.

Debbie turned to me, put her hand on my shoulder, and said, "We have a serious problem."

"Right. We need to go get him," I responded without hesitation.

Apparently, Tim had gotten to the aid station after the cutoff—the point at which the aid station closes and runners aren't permitted to continue their race. Not only that, but Tim also seemed a bit out of it and delirious when he arrived. Hearing this, Debbie was furious that the aid station captain not only let Tim leave in the state he was in, but also permitted him to go on after the cutoff time. Aid station captains were supposed to inform race HQ of any runner who arrived past the cutoff time, and we would help make the decision of whether to let the runner continue or inform them that their race was over. Race HQ hadn't been told about Tim's missing the cutoff time. Apparently, after resting for a bit at the aid station, Tim had left without telling a soul.

We also learned that Tim had gone off the trail in the dark the previous night and made a few wrong turns, which is not uncommon when racing an ultra-marathon. A race this long may take several days to finish, and runners need to be able to navigate in complete darkness at times and might even need to take sleeping breaks.

The good news though was that Tim was less than eight miles from the Heavenly aid station. According to his spot tracker, he kept turning around and heading in the opposite direction every few miles, indicating he didn't have any idea where he was or where he was going. Because of his frequent turnarounds, we were concerned that he might not be lucid and wondered if he was properly fueled or just simply lost.

We had no way to communicate with him—we could only see where he was and where he was going. We had no information about his food or water supply or if he had proper clothing with him. Both Debbie and I knew Tim—he was an experienced long-distance ultrarunner, running distances well over 26.2 miles (the marathon distance) on a regular basis—and this fact eased some of our concerns.

We immediately contacted the El Dorado County sheriff's office and informed them of the situation to see if they could help us with the search-and-rescue mission. However, things weren't dire from their point of view just yet. Technically, he wasn't missing and there were no reports of his being in serious danger.

Once we realized the local authorities were going to be of minimal help, we took matters into our own hands. We were going to rescue Tim as soon as possible.

As much as I actually wanted to save Tim, I also wanted the

challenge. Being an experienced trail runner myself, it made sense for me to go after him. Plus, I knew the trails better than almost all of the runners, having spent so much time marking the race route. When I told Debbie I was going after him, she agreed right away and handed me a two-way radio so I could stay in contact with her and Paul. I jumped into my van and took off on Route 50 toward Heavenly, barreling down the road. I only had a few hours of daylight left. I hoped I could run up the trail, find Tim, and bring him back safely and be a hero.

Tunnel Creek was about a forty-five-minute drive from the Heavenly Ski Resort, where Tim had last checked in. When I arrived there, the aid station had been closed for hours, and it was completely abandoned aside from a dozen trash bags, folded-up tables, and the head medic, Larry, who had already been informed about what we knew of Tim's condition. He'd been expecting me.

Larry was a heavier-set guy who always wore his red medic shirt with the white cross on the front and back. He loved being a medic and was always concerned about every runner, but in this particular case, I could see the concern written all over him: sweat beads stood out on his forehead, his voice was unusually serious, and he was working hard to maintain a calm and collected demeanor. Seeing me, he opened the trunk of his brown Subaru station wagon and asked if I needed anything. In the cargo space, there were, among other things, a bottle of water and a granola bar. I grabbed them both and stuffed them into my pocket. We agreed that Larry would wait for Tim and me there unless he heard otherwise.

Time was of the essence; I had to find Tim before nightfall. The lower the sun sank into the horizon, the higher the chance was that he would have to spend the night in the woods, potentially putting his health in danger. Nodding goodbye to Larry, I raced up the hill, the two-way radio in my left hand and the bottle of water in my right. My adrenaline was already pumping.

I stayed in constant contact with Paul over the radio as we tried to pinpoint Tim's exact coordinates. Unfortunately, he was moving farther and farther away from the Heavenly aid station, where I'd started. My hope of finding Tim within the first thirty minutes quickly faded. I cruised up the mountain following the trail I had previously marked. Ski lifts towered above me, tall pine trees stood to my left and right, and dry, light-brown dirt crunched under my feet.

Before I knew it, I had covered over seven miles in my rescue operation. Considering that Tim already had over seventy miles on his legs from this race, he was moving surprisingly quickly. According to Paul on the other end of the radio, I wasn't gaining much on him, and I was growing frustrated.

Finally, in the distance, I saw a few people on the trail. *Maybe it's Tim*, I thought hopefully. There wouldn't be many hikers this deep into the trail this late in the day; perhaps someone else had found Tim and was helping him.

Once I got closer though, I saw that this was not the case. Instead, they were just a couple in their early forties.

"Have either of you seen a runner with trekking poles and a small backpack who looked lost?" I inquired, trying to catch my breath.

"Nope. We haven't seen anyone in quite some time," the woman responded.

I relayed this information back to race HQ, and it was not received well. *Where the hell are you, Tim?*

I briefly explained the situation to them, and the hikers were kind enough to offer me more water. I hadn't anticipated being out there this long, and I had already consumed the granola bar and most of the water I had brought with me. Thanking the hikers, I continued on, running farther up into the mountains and screaming Tim's name as loudly as I could.

Tim was tall and lanky. In his real life on the coast of Oregon, he was a school principal. I'd gotten to know him and his wife, Pamela, back in Washington. Tim was an accomplished ultrarunner in his own right and wasn't a stranger to the trails or to this race. Tim's experience was comforting, but it was also concerning, because he normally wouldn't have put himself in such a dire situation. He knew better.

As time passed and I went farther up the trail, I was starting to get concerned for myself. I lacked proper clothes and supplies, and as I ran deeper into the mountains, the two-way radio became increasingly spotty. The dense pine trees now blanketed the landscape, and all I could hear was my breath, my feet pounding along the trail, and coyotes howling in the distance. I was more than ten miles into my search—way beyond my and HQ's expectations. The sun was getting low, and so were my chances of finding Tim. At some point, I would eventually have to decide whether to turn back or keep going.

I knew the course was well marked with dragons, in this particular area, because I was the one who had helped mark it. All Tim had to do was follow the dragons on the trail. It was so easy. So why couldn't he do it?

As I flew along the trail, I considered the irony of the fact that I was the one on this rescue mission. It's not that I wasn't capable of running and finding Tim in the middle of nowhere. No, what was ironic was that I had never been able to follow the course markings in my own life—the life that had sent me wandering on yet another journey, even when it seemed like I should finally be content. All I had to do in life was follow the dragons that were so prominently displayed. But I hadn't. Instead, I so often chased after the wrong ones or missed them completely. For years, I had assumed I was going in the right direction, but I was wrong. I thought that if Tim had known this about me, he might have wished it were someone else chasing after him. Even though I knew exactly where I was going on the trail, I felt more lost than I ever had in my life, and now, someone else's life was in my hands.

My thoughts were interrupted by Paul's static-laced voice over the radio: "Kyle, if you don't see Tim in the next mile or so, just head back."

I stopped running for a moment and looked up at the empty trail, feeling somewhat defeated. I pressed the radio button to reply, "I'm not coming back without Tim."

I pushed forward. The spark within me flashed hot; I knew that I'd meant what I said. All of a sudden, finding Tim felt not only like the most important thing about this race, but the most important thing in my life. It felt like everything had led me to this point: the trauma of my childhood, my substance abuse as a teenager and twenty-something, my inability to find and keep healthy relationships, both platonic and romantic. I had made a series of choices that had put me back on the right path. I had found my sense of confidence. I had channeled that spark that was always there, and I was following the path I felt I needed to follow. Maybe it was all for this moment: to find Tim and save him. To bring him back to his—no, to *our*—community.

It wasn't until I was about eleven miles in that I saw a figure stumbling down the trail. "Tim!" I screamed, and he replied in the affirmative that it was him. He was relieved that I had found him; I had never seen somebody so happy to see me in my life.

"Kyle? Kyle? Is that you? Oh thank god," he said, overcome with emotion.

"Are you done running away from me?" I said with a smile as I embraced him.

He had water with him, and he seemed to be able to move okay. In fact, he was in amazing spirits. He just kept thanking me. It warmed my heart and I couldn't stop smiling about the fact that I'd finally done something right on this adventure and I was actually needed.

Now the issue was getting back safely with Tim. We were too far out to just turn around; it would be dark long before we got back. We needed to find an alternate route to a trailhead and to civilization. Luckily, we were still able to communicate with HQ, and they navigated us down the mountain and to another trailhead, where Larry, the medic, had been told to be and was waiting for us. To my surprise, Tim was coherent and able to move at a good pace. We made it down the mountain as the sun sank below the horizon where Larry was sitting on a boulder in the trailhead parking lot.

Toward the end of the race, snow hit the mountains, even though it was early September. We started to get concerned for the runners, who were probably not prepared for this. It had been in the eighties during the day, but now it dropped well below freezing at night. Thankfully, there were no incidents.

I took on the responsibility of getting all the finishers' final times and photos so I could post them on the race Facebook page. It was tough getting the time of every runner who crossed the finish line, because they came in so far apart. It was hard to get any sleep. Debbie, Robin, Paul, and Brian were all with me at the finish line with me, greeting runners as they completed their journey. To make it easier, we pulled our vehicles up beside the finish and slept whenever we could. When we heard someone shout, *"Runner,"* we would all jump out of our vehicles and make sure there was someone there to greet and congratulate each runner. Imagine coming to the end of a race at three thirty in the morning with nobody there to see it; we wanted to assure that wouldn't happen. We had chairs and tables set up with food, water, heaters, and blankets for the runners. Just like in Washington, they also got their own personalized pizzas.

The day after the race, we had a party at race HQ. There was an upstairs at the ski resort lodge with a kitchen and a dining space that we were allowed to hang out in and have an award ceremony. It was good to get everyone together to talk about their experiences—not just the runners, but also their families, the crew, and the volunteers who'd experienced their triumph as well. People were laughing and crying, and everyone was having a good time.

The next morning, we finished packing up the trailer. We also had the opportunity to go through the drop bags that had been left behind. It was a stated and known policy that whatever wasn't claimed before the runners left was fair game to the volunteers. People left running poles, shoes, jackets, phones, and food. I was surprised by how many people just left expensive race gear behind. We went through whatever hadn't been claimed and took what we wanted. The rest, we either donated or trashed.

Now that the race was over, I needed to decide what I was going to do next. Others around me were contemplating the same question. Stick around in Tahoe? Head out to Moab? For me, it was between staying here for a while or heading back to Ohio. The decision seemed especially fraught: Should I keep wandering, keep chasing that thing that I never seemed to catch? Or did I trust myself to return back home to Ohio, the place of so many demons and bad memories?

I really liked the trail running community. But I wondered whether it was something sustainable for someone like me. I had my apartment I was paying for, and I didn't think I was ready to uproot my life completely and move out west like I had done when I was much younger and followed Brad out to San Francisco. What I really liked, I realized, was the experience of making these friends and being seen by them in a way that I wasn't seen by anyone back in Cleveland. I was a bit of a novelty to them, sure, but they took me for who I was and liked me for it. That alone felt like a powerful thing to take away from the experience, even if nothing else came from it.

So many ultrarunners are recovering alcoholics or addicts who use the trail as medicine. Some of them get themselves into trouble by swapping one addiction for another. Most, though, use ultrarunning as an outlet. I'm sure they're all running away from something like I was. But the funny thing was, I was starting to feel like I didn't need to commit to it 100 percent in order to feel its healing powers. This community of runners felt so strong because we all relied on each other to survive and thrive in the rugged conditions out on the mountain, working together the whole time, the runners all bonding shoulder to shoulder on the trail. But the community was only a community in the broadest sense—running brought us together, but because everyone was always moving on, it was difficult for anyone to really form deep relationships with one another.

It felt more like I had gained access to a community that would always be available to me, a way to work through my issues and fears that would always be accessible, regardless of where I was or who I was around. True, the streets of Cleveland were nothing like the Cascade Mountains. But I would soon learn that there were trail running communities everywhere, including the Cuyahoga Valley National Park. Maybe, I thought, I didn't need to live the dirtbag runner lifestyle out west to find my tribe. Maybe it was right there with PJ, Chris, Baby, and this new version of Kyle who I was beginning to like.

EPILOGUE: HERE I AM

Every year, I take a few trips with my best friends. Some are mostly social, like the trip we take every August to a music festival in Challis, Idaho or, in November, to Cozumel, Mexico to go scuba diving. But every October, I go to Titusville, Pennsylvania to run the Oil Creek 50K trail race with PJ, Chris, and sometimes Baby. It's become our own little tradition.

Titusville is an old oil town known as the birthplace of the American oil industry, where the first ever commercial oil well was established in 1859. It was a thriving center of industry for a time, though now it's a small town of around 5,000 residents. The race headquarters are at the middle school, so organizers have to wait until the fall football schedule is released to set a date for the race. Once it's announced in February, there's a huge rush to book one of the few nearby hotels—if you don't do it that same day, you might end up sleeping in a tent outside of the school or on the school's gym floor. The registration fills up fast, too—I usually sign up our entire group as soon as the registration window opens up in March, so no one else has to worry about it. Best case scenario is when registration opens up while we're all over at PJ's on Sunday morning for coffee and peanuts—another tradition.

Last year, it was just me and PJ running, with Chris and his girlfriend Abby joining us for support. PJ lives within a mile of me in Cleveland so he and I drove down together, chatting or listening to a podcast the whole way down. He doesn't open up much, normally, so I always treasure the opportunity to get him sharing more about his life on our long drive. I met PJ before anyone else in the CEC and he introduced me to Chris and Baby. Once we arrived, we picked up our bibs, dropped our bags at the Quality Inn, and met Chris and Abby at Fat Chad's Tap and Steakhouse—our usual spot. Like a lot of other ultras, Oil Creek provides a pasta dinner the night before the race. The spaghetti dinner isn't our style because we like to meet up with other runners at Fat Chad's every year to share war stories of past Oil Creek races and other ultras. As I've gotten older, I've expanded my palate and am not as strict with my diet—although I still try to eat a healthy whole foods plant based diet. Everyone ate until they were stuffed and headed back to the hotel for bed.

At the start line the next morning, I went sprinting out of the gate as I usually do. PJ stayed back—though he's a strong runner, he always sets his sights on finishing, not winning, the race. I, on the other hand, always want to compete. Last year, there were 250 other runners in the 50K, and I was determined to keep my streak of top-five finishes. Chris and Abby met me at the aid station around mile fourteen to cheer me on and give me my electrolyte drink; seeing them gave me the boost I needed to keep pace.

Sprinting to the finish line is my favorite part of the race because I love hearing everyone clapping and yelling and cheering me on. There was a big crowd this past year, and they brought me in with gusto as I claimed my fourth-place finish—the same as last year. Exhausted, I plopped down in a chair and waited to cheer PJ in.

Post-race is my favorite time at Oil Creek. We have our own traditions: First, we go to the Elks club to debrief about the race, eat popcorn, and chat with some of the locals who are always amazed that we can run that far. From there, we went to Titusville Iron Works Tap House. Last year, there was a Bon Jovi cover band rocking the big warehouse bar, packed with locals. We danced and danced until my legs literally gave out—I was exhausted from the race. After the concert, we headed back to the hotel for one more tradition: Chris and I stripping the sheets off the beds to have a toga party. After a few laughs, it was off to bed. We had a long drive back to Cleveland in the morning.

No one in the Cleveland Explorers Club really thinks of themselves as a hardcore ultrarunner. Maybe I'm not either—I love the sport, love the healthy outlet it gives me, and love meeting people through races across the country, but a little part of me always felt different from the "dirtbag runners" I came to know out west. I definitely wasn't built to be as transient as some of the others. But also, even for those runners who had built their entire lives around ultras, it was difficult for everyone to form deep relationships because everyone was always moving on. We were all there, but maybe not all fully present.

When I came back from my trip, I felt like I was on firmer footing; the dread I normally felt when I returned to Ohio wasn't quite as bad. Maybe, I thought, I didn't need a complete escape, to throw myself into something 100 percent. In many ways, despite all the baggage I would always have in Ohio, what I was searching for with my trip out west was waiting for me right in my own backyard.

With Chris, P.J., and Baby, I'd found something like a surrogate family, a group of people who were almost always positive and who almost always make me feel good, supporting me and pulling the best version of myself out of me. Around them, I always feel like I can be myself—I don't need to put on a show or conform to any particular way of thinking. Most importantly, they're there for me when I need them: On birthdays, they buy me cards and a cake. During breakups, they're there to commiserate or distract me, whichever I need. They've taught me what true friendship means, and I do my best to be there in the same way they're there for me.

Finding your tribe is so important—and your true tribe isn't just obsessed with the same things as you but understands you to your core, accepting you as you are.

At different points in my life, I thought I might be a juvenile delinquent or prisoner; a bartender; a high-powered lawyer at a big firm; and a dirtbag ultrarunner wandering around the country in search of kinship and adrenaline. But I've become someone so much better than any of those versions I'd imagined for myself.

I'm lucky—beyond lucky. The best part of my day is getting up before the sun rises and knowing that I'm going to meet my friends at 5:30 a.m. to run.

———————————◆———————————

Triple B, of course, has never really changed. There was a time after his mother passed that it seemed like he might. When we moved back to Ohio as kids, his mother would babysit me and my siblings. I didn't have the same bond with her as I did with my own grandmother, but she treated us well, and I remember playing with blocks in her guest room. She had been a church-going woman, and when she passed, Triple B started going to church, too—

something that he'd never done before, even when Mom would take us kids. He seemed to want to become a better person, at least for a little while. That was short-lived, and eventually he just went back to his old ways.

I see Mom once a year now, when the family rents a cottage in Lakeside, Ohio for the 4th of July. It's nice because my brother, my sister, and all their kids are there and Triple B never is, so it feels like a real family vacation—a nice one, where no one is fighting and everyone gets along.

My trip out west clarified a lot for me, made me realize just how traumatic many parts of my childhood had been—and how horribly I still felt, thinking back on Triple B's abuse. When I got back home, I decided that I was going to write about my adventure because I wanted to memorialize it. As I wrote about my adventure, for some reason, I started to write about how I was raised. Suddenly, on the paper, everything Triple B did to me was coming out and I was finally coming to the realization of what happened to me, the impact it had on my life, and why I made some of the decisions I have made. Writing about my past made me realize for the first time that I was abused. Not a victim, just something that happened to me and knowing what happened, I can do something about it. It was a sense of relief and empowerment. I decided it was time to discuss this with Mom. I took a piece of paper with what I wanted to say to her just like I'd done during drug rehab. Not confront her, but talk to her about what happened to me and my siblings as we grew up. I asked Mom to meet me at my sister's house in Columbus, and she asked me whether Triple B should come, too. I told her he couldn't.

We sat down on my sister's couch, I pulled out my paper, and before I could even start talking, the tears started flowing. Eventually

I got out everything I wanted to say: That my siblings and I had been raised by an abusive man, that I didn't want her to call him my father anymore, that keeping this charade up was killing me inside. She was crying, too, by the end. It was one of the hardest things I've ever done.

I had this dream in my head that this might heal things between Mom and me—maybe even help heal things between me and Triple B. At the very least, I'd hoped it might bring Mom and me closer. If anything, though, it pushed us farther apart. Coming to terms with what I'd told her would mean she would have to come to terms with bringing a monster into our lives that tormented and abused her kids—and she couldn't face that.

We tried to talk it out a few times after that, but we never really moved forward. I knew that at the end of every conversation she wanted me to tell her that it wasn't so bad, that he was a good father after all. But it wasn't true, and I couldn't say it. Eventually, she stopped asking about it and went back to pretending that everything was fine.

I know she is hurting inside, and I wish I could take her pain away. But, I've also come to the realization that I can't change anyone who doesn't want to change. And in any case, I need to heal myself first.

I didn't write this book to vilify anybody—not even Triple B. I wanted to share my experience and hoped that others might be able to gain something from it. There are a lot of moments where I know I come off as a jerk—looking back now, I can't help but be frustrated with the younger version of myself who took so long to learn from his mistakes. I wanted to be true to myself and the reader and tell my story, bad parts and all. I'm only human. Clearly I don't have it all figured out. I was—and still am—trying to do the best I can.

I kept trying to escape and find happiness and meaning in new places and in unhealthy relationships or with drugs and alcohol, not knowing they wouldn't cure me. I kept trying to prove everyone wrong, and when I couldn't, I ended up unhappy. I needed to face myself and realize that if I just kept running away from what had happened to me, I would suffer the same fate for the rest of my life no matter where I was. The easiest way for me to come to terms with what I had been through and to heal was to share my story.

It was a long road to get to a place where I've felt healthy enough to share my story with others. I saw about a half-dozen therapists before I found one that practiced a style—Internal Family Systems therapy (IFS)—that helped me come to terms with my childhood. Along with therapy, journaling, exercise, healthy eating, goal setting, reading, and changing my relationship with alcohol have all been key to me in maintaining a healthy lifestyle and continuing to improve, to help keep that spark inside me alive. Not to mention Booker, a seven-year-old, eighty-five pound, goldendoodle who I call my best friend. He's with me almost all the time now, providing me so much comfort and unconditional love.

Obviously, a huge tenet in my life has been to always keep pushing forward and not give up. But what I found was actually most important in my adventure—and in my life—was that the people I surrounded myself with ended up shaping my life, for better or for worse. I believe I am better off alone than with negative people. Success is subjective, and I believe everyone needs to blaze their own path to happiness and fulfillment, not follow the trail others tell them to follow. I know I'm not the only one who has felt that spark inside of them. In my case, it was a spark that was just as likely to have burned down everything around me as it was to illuminate the path in front of me.

Life isn't always going to be what I expect it to be, and true fulfillment is intangible. Instead, what matters most is my continued growth and appreciation for life as it unfolds along the way.

I know now where I belong: wherever I am.

ACKNOWLEDGEMENTS

My sister, my brother Kate and Kirk — I love you all more than you will ever know. I'm thankful each day you're in my life.

Mom, I understand. I love you so much.

My Nephews Trenten, Owen, William and Nolan I love you.

To the connection, Mary Kate, Wes, and the rest of my family, thank you for making me laugh on a daily basis and being there for me when I need you.

David Schnurman, you have impacted my life more than I can express with words. You gave me the strength and courage to believe in myself and go after what I want in life. I know this book wouldn't have existed if I'd never met you. Micah Bochart, principles and morals are what I aspire to live up to. Frank Furbacher, Michele Richman, and Sigalle Barness—I couldn't have asked to work with better people. Although we may have grown apart as the years passed, I hold fond memories of seeing you all, every day at the office. Thank you for giving me something to look forward to on a daily basis. Frank Bastone, thank you for taking a chance on me—you've changed the trajectory of my life more than you will ever know.

Tom Brady (the teacher), Victor Bishop, and Sister Collette, it would have been easier for all of you not to take the time out of your day to talk some sense into me. It may not have seemed like it at the time, but I heard every word you said and I listened.

Brett Blomme, Chris Dolen, and Maury Koffman—thank

you for your friendship, guidance, and teaching me how to be successful in school.

To Second Sole in Lakewood, Ohio. It's because of you I've met my life long friends and have gotten through many races.

Uncle Ray, thank you for opening your home to me and giving me experiences I never would have had if it wasn't for you – especially Idaho and Cozumel.

Cousin Eric and Jenna, thanks for watching Booker when I'm on my crazy adventures and for the sitting room.

My editor Justin Brouckaert, I appreciate the time and patience you took to work on my book. The questions you asked brought out so much more in me than I thought I had to share. Nuno Moreira, my cover designer, thank you for creating a cover I never would have had without you.

To Chris Moore, PJ Moore, and Eric Baby Mooney, (aka the CEC) -Thank you for being more than just my friends. I wouldn't want to share the trails and life with anyone else.

To my friends who were in my life for a season or two - I am grateful for you.

Everyone at Town-B Press for believing in me.

John Mustard – we miss you so much. Finally, Booker Brooks— thank you for believing in me, always. I don't know what I would do without you.

KYLE V ROBINSON is a graduate of Kent State University and Western Michigan University Cooley Law School. Kyle, currently, resides in Ohio with his dog Booker. You can find him running on trails and at: kylevrobinson.com.